"Nancy offers a unique pe energy surrounding us all. Armed with the information presented herein, you'll be well on your way to manifesting the power of the cosmic energy in your own life."

—Chris Pierre, procurement manager

"Reading this book was truly inspirational. It's remarkable how surrounding yourself and loved ones in positive energy can have such a huge impact. These simple changes have made me more aware and have impacted how I move through life. This really is a game changer, Nancy, and I hope your message reaches many!"

—Carrie Hummel, professional hair designer

"How to use universal energy changed the way I viewed the world. It helped me see the energy in everything around me and how that affected my daily life. Nancy taught me how I could use that energy to be a happier and more fulfilled. This book inspired and taught me so much!"

—Crystal Pierre, marketing specialist

"I really enjoyed your book! So many people take for granted what they have! They don't pay attention to what God has put in front of them. God puts ideas and direction in our lives every day. I agree, they need to Wake Up! Myself included."

—Stacey Kneer, businesswoman

"Nancy Yearout does an exceptional job teaching people how to use the power of thoughts, prayers and energy to better their lives. This book puts the power we have to better ourselves into perspective. Ask and you shall receive. Put good energy and thoughts out to the Universe and it will make a difference in your everyday life."

—Samantha Bohmier, account manager

"I found this book very enlightening. The power of energy is amazing! This book helps you navigate through life with tools on how to get rid of the negative energy and keep the positive energy flowing."

—Nita Diem, certified mortgage broker

"I found this book to be informative, engaging, and insightful. The author has made it easy to refer back to when guidance or refresher is needed. I definitely had some Aha moments."

—Joni Ulibarri, dental assistant

WAKE UP!

THE UNIVERSE IS SPEAKING TO YOU

Learn to Use Universal
Energy to Change Your Life

NANCY E. YEAROUT

ENERGY GIRL
PUBLISHING

This book is dedicated to the love of my life, my husband, Mark. Thank you for always standing beside me, believing in me, and being my biggest cheerleader. You are my best friend and my bicycle-riding partner. I love you forever!

Thank you to my daughters, Crystal and Samantha, for supporting me; I love you for that! You have both grown into smart, lovely ladies. You've become great moms, and I am proud of you both!

To my sister Judy, who has gone to be with the Lord, you have influenced me with your kind soul more than you know. I feel your presence often when a song that we used to sing comes into my head. I miss you.

Thanks to the Lord for our grandchildren, Xander, Isabelle, and Bennett Cooper; you keep us going with your bright eyes and happy smiles.

And to my parents, Newton and June McConnaughey, and my sisters Lizbeth and Julie, I love you, and may the Lord bless you with His energy.

Contents

Preface

I was in my thirties when I began to pay attention to the Universal Energy and how it works. I realized that the energy of the people whom I was associating with and the energy of my surroundings were affecting me. The energy, whether negative or positive, had a great influence on my happiness, health, and well-being. I started to pay attention to what was occurring all around me. God our Creator was showing me how the Universe worked, how he set it up for us. I was being shown the Laws of the Universe. This was the beginning of my spiritual journey.

I paid attention and began using this energy as it was intended, for our benefit. My curiosity regarding the Universal Energy and how our Creator designed it has led me to research and acquire many invaluable spiritual lessons thus far. These are simple things that God put in place to make our lives easier.

Within these pages you will learn how to work with the energy to your advantage. You will read my story and how I use this energy to enhance my business and personal life. I will teach you how to use affirmations to achieve your goals in life. I cast light upon the power of prayer and its energy benefits to all who believe. I make clear how energy can cause wellness or illness in your body and how to clear the negative energy contributing to health issues. I will show you how the messages that the Universe sends us will keep you on the right path. I discuss the angels and how they assist us while on our life's journey. Throughout this book I share many life lessons acquired along the way. I am confident that the information that I share in these pages will bring happiness, prosperity, and a more fulfilled life to all who read this and use the energy as it was intended.

As you learn to work with the Universal Energy, you will begin to realize the power this energy holds. You will understand that as humans, we possess much more ability than many of us may have realized or are utilizing.

We have the strength and the capability as individuals and as the collective to change the energy here on this planet. As more and more people begin working with the Universal Energy and projecting positive vibrations, our lives and our surroundings will shine more brightly for us as a people. We actually have an opportunity to make a difference in this vast Universe with our good energy vibrations. Now that's big!

Maybe there is more to our purpose here on earth than you once thought. We, as the Universal Energy pioneers, must think of the possibilities that lie ahead and how that energy will benefit our future generations. Our good energy travels out into the Universe, only to be returned to us tenfold. Good vibrations create more good vibrations. It's infectious! All of the good vibrations that we send out, the

Universe naturally bounces back to us. It's as the old saying goes, "You only get what you give."

The returning energy creates harmony and balance for all of us who project good energy. The planet earth receives the good vibes, too, and will balance itself. Bonus! We thrive in peace and harmony. This is why it is important for you to learn about Universal Energy and how to use it. This gift is for your benefit, and for all the others that will follow.

Acknowledgments

I would like to thank the Lord for guiding my hand and my mind as I wrote this book.

I wish to acknowledge Naomi Kreger, a spiritual teacher and a wise soul. Naomi taught me to have faith in myself and in the Lord.

I am grateful to the people who opened up and allowed me to tell their real life stories in this book. Many thanks to Holly, Greg, Lana & Joe, and Rebecca. I know that your shared experiences will make a difference in many people's lives.

Thank you to all of the great inspirational leaders that have come before me for sharing their healing knowledge. I acknowledge all of the great teachers of our time.

Thank you to my publicist, Sara Sgarlat, for keeping me on my path, and to Jonathan Friedman's skilled hand at creating a fabulous cover for the book. May the Lord bless you with His energy.

—Nancy E. Yearout

Everything is energy and that's all there is to it. Match the frequency of the reality you want and you cannot help but get that reality. It can be no other way. This is not philosophy. This is physics.

—Unknown (popularly attributed to Albert Einstein)

Chapter 1

How Energy Affects Your Everyday Life

MANY OF US ARE intuitive, myself included. I am able to feel the energy of most people upon our first encounter. Everyone's different. Some of us have high energy levels, vibrating at a higher frequency, while others remain at a lower frequency, mellow and more constant. Some people have such positive energy that they are similar to bright lights that shine. When you look at them, you can actually see the light in their eyes. The light comes from God and shines from within. It's amazing how you can feel this joyful positive energy emanating from someone when you first meet them.

On the other side of the spectrum, negative energy can be felt very harshly in people, too. Negative energy will cause much havoc in our lives when we are exposed to it. Negative energy holds just as much power as positive energy does and should be recognized equally. For example, have you ever encountered a person whom you were just not comfortable being around? Maybe you felt uneasy or apprehensive when you were in the same room. You were experiencing their negative energy field. Let me be clear: there are evil people in this world, and they hold an abundant amount of negative dark energy. These people are oftentimes called "Energy Vampires." They are not able to produce their own light energy, so they steal yours. Energy Vampires can be charming on the outside but negative on the inside. They disguise themselves well, as a chameleon would do. For example, you may encounter a new person at a party, and after coming into contact with them, you feel drained of your energy. You may even become nauseated. Another scenario is that a friend may be going through a breakup or difficult time in their life and they come to you for support. When they leave, they are fine, and you are drained of your positive energy; they have stolen your good energy for themselves. In most cases this is not done intentionally—folks do not realize that they are doing this to you. This is, however, an Energy Vampire. Often the people who are the closest to you will drain your energy field without your ever realizing that they are doing it. It is up to each of us to be aware of the people that surround us. We should be aware of the people we associate with on a daily basis, because they have an effect on our energy field.

Have you ever visited a place where you just did not feel comfortable? Did it make you so uneasy that you chose not to stay in that place or return there? The place holds negative energy in its space, and your intuition has picked up on the frequency of the energy. Possibly, angry people lived there or a violent death occurred at that location. The negative energy remains etched in that space, and the events are imprinted there for all time. This has been known to happen on old battlefields. The old energy of the battle remains on the grounds. The energy is imprinted on the land where the fighting and killing took place. You can feel this energy when you walk the land.

The same is true when you experience positive energy. When you walk into a room and it feels good, you want to stay there; your intuition kicks in and says, "I am comfortable here." The place makes you smile and is one where you feel joyful and want to return. You are experiencing positive energy. Good vibes, as people often say.

Before I realized that God had orchestrated the Universe in this manner, I was under the delusion that I held the power to determine what occurred around me. I believed that I was smart enough to control everything in my world. I learned after many trials and much error that we are not in control of anything. Our Creator is. That was a real wake-up call for me, especially since I was such a control freak.

What I have come to realize is that energy and how it affects our everyday life seems to go unnoticed by most of us. I think, as a society, we have not been taught to recognize that positive and negative energy exist, let alone the fact that energy has a huge impact on our everyday existence. I have been fortunate to learn about Universal Energy and the effects it has on us. Once I began to recognize this fact, I became aware that I could change my life for the better. What I have learned is that energy is power. This power is here for us to use. Whether we use it for good or for evil is entirely up to us.

3

Energy is spoken about in the Bible many times, so I refer to scriptures from one of the oldest books on the planet to give you a clear understanding of how the energy was intended to work for us:

> *He is the one we proclaim, admonishing and teaching every-*
> *one with all wisdom, so that we may present everyone fully*
> *mature in Christ. To this end I strenuously contend with all*
> *the energy Christ so powerfully works in me.*
> —Colossians 1:28–29

This scripture clearly states that energy is in your soul—the Christ energy, if you so choose.

Let's talk about energy and how it affects our health. In a positive place, surrounded by happy, positive people you tend to feel the same way. The energy is good, and you can feel it in the air; it's contagious. This positive energy stays with you throughout the day and affects how you interact with everyone you meet and how they react to you. It's the power of attraction. Positive energy attracts more positive energy. When you encounter a negative person, be careful, as their energy may rub off on you just as easily. When you come across such a situation, the best thing to do is to distance yourself from that person. They will bring you down to their energy level.

Unfortunately, I have experienced more than my share of ugly energy in my lifetime. Negative people do not like positive, happy people who are full of good energy and light. Many dark people among us are angry and hateful souls. You need to acknowledge that they exist. Negative people do not want to see happy, positive folks enjoying their lives. Their goal is to drain your positive energy from you so that you can be as angry and unhappy as they are. There's that old saying, "Misery loves company." This statement is true. The best advice I can give you is to stay away from negative people. Their negative energy is toxic to you.

Sadly, I have observed many couples who are in an unhealthy relationship. One of the partners appears happy, healthy, and fulfilled, while the other is sad, drained, and unhealthy-looking. One is draining the energy from the other, stealing the other person's light. There have been many books written about this. As I mentioned earlier, these people are called Energy Vampires. What you need to understand is that no one can steal your light if you don't allow them to, but sometimes this is happening and you are not even realizing it. Wake Up! Pay attention to your surroundings and the people whom you are surrounding yourself with. The best solution is to stay away from Energy Vampires completely. The dark is attracted to the light as a moth is attracted to a light bulb.

This scenario occurs frequently in the workplace. Jealousy and ego are the main reasons this behavior occurs. Unfortunately, the majority of the time people don't even realize what is happening to them until it is too late and they're drained of their good energy. We become physically ill when this occurs.

A person's light can dim from an abusive relationship or from a bully in the workplace after the person's consistent exposure to the negativity over time. The person becomes drained of all of their positive energy, resulting in lower energy vibrations. The lower energy frequency will bring the person's immune system down. This low energy level in the body leaves an open door for disease to enter. The result, if not cleared, is sickness and disease within the body. I believe bad energy is a huge contributing factor to many of the health issues we are experiencing today.

It's sad to say, but most all of us know someone who has been afflicted with cancer, Alzheimer's disease, dementia, or some other type of fatal or debilitating health issue. As the years have passed, I have recognized that we all know someone who has died from some form of cancer. Why have these illnesses become so prevalent in our society today? For a long period, I felt that the increase of disease was a result of additives to our food or in our water supply. While I do believe that the food and drink that we put into our bodies determine our general health, I feel strongly that the stressful environment that we inhabit and the negative energy we are exposed to are the largest contributors to disease in the body. We tend to internalize the negative energy, thus interrupting the good flow. As a result, health issues are created. Our parents and grandparents did not experience the amount of stress and pressure in life that we do today. The young people of our world have an enormous amount of stress on them. The energy of peer pressure alone can cause havoc to the body's energy fields. Oftentimes this negative energy is internalized, as the young don't know how to rid themselves of it. As a result, many of our young are victims of low energy fields, a condition that may cause sickness and disease in their bodies.

After revealing this information to you, I feel it imperative for you to understand that when you are around negativity for a long period, the negative energy will eventually consume you. I cannot emphasize this fact enough! This is something you need to pay attention to as you go through your life. Be aware of the energy around you at all times, as the energy affects all aspects of your world.

You, or someone you know, may be in this situation. There can be various scenarios where this can occur—living with a negative family member or a friend, for example. If you are in this situation, or ever find yourself in this situation, know that it's unhealthy for you mentally and physically to remain. You should remove yourself from the situation immediately. What happens when you remain exposed to negative energy for any length of time is that the energy gets into your body and gets stuck in your muscle, your tissue, and your bones. It also gets into your car and your home and rubs off on all the people you meet. Just because you cannot see the bad energy does not mean it isn't present. The negative energy that is causing problems can be cleared from a person and their space. But when you don't know how to clear the energy, the negativity will remain and build.

Another way you can receive negative energy without even realizing it is when people think negative thoughts and speak negative words about you. Yes, gossip. The energy of our thoughts and that of our words, whether positive or negative, each have a specific vibration. They will reach whomever they are intended for. The vibration of the spoken word is strong as it travels out into the Universe. The power lies with the energy of the intention. The negativity that a person can send by their spoken words or their thoughts reaches the intended party and causes an imbalance in their energy fields. This negativity drains away the good energy that is naturally in their soul.

One of my goals in writing this book is to teach you how to shield yourself from bad energy and how to clear your energy fields. I will give specific suggestions in chapter 3 on how you can protect yourself. If you are going to understand the energy and use it for your benefit, you will need to understand your own energy fields and what each one's function is. You may be familiar with the seven energy fields in your body. If not, they are called the *chakras*. In chapter 2, I have included the basics for your reference so that you can understand each energy field, where it is located, and its function in your body.

Chapter 2

The Energy Fields in Your Body

THE FIRST TYPE OF energy field I'm going to share with you is called the *chakra*. If you are not acquainted with it, the word *chakra* originates from the Indian language and means "wheel" or "disk." There are seven energy centers in our bodies that are spinning with energy. Each energy field, or chakra, pushes the vital energy through our bodies. This essential energy is often called *chi* or *prana*. The chi energy spins in a spiral motion along your spine. This energy is providing you with good health, vitality, wisdom, and intuitiveness from the Divine.

There may have been a time in your life that you felt energy entering into the top of your head. It feels like a tingling sensation. This energy center is called the *crown chakra*. The energy from our Creator moves down through the body though the crown chakra. As the energy spirals downward, it is rotating in a counterclockwise motion. The chakras are vital to our life force.

When one or more of your chakras are out of balance, this means your energy fields are out of balance. When this happens, it affects your health and general well-being. Negative energy can get stuck in the energy fields in your body unless you release it. When one of your energy fields is out of balance, it is most likely infested with negative, dirty energy. There is imbalance in the body. The chakras hold the key to our good health and happiness.

I predict that someday we will go to the doctor and the medical professional will scan our energy fields to find out what ailment afflicts us, much like when we have an MRI. A simple energy scan may be able to prevent disease in the early stages. For this very reason, I am a huge believer in making sure your chakras are balanced and clear. Each chakra is associated with a color. Each color holds a unique meaning relating to that particular energy center within your body. I have included the seven chakras here so that you can begin to recognize any issues within your own body. You will see that each chakra has a different function throughout the body. There are several ways to clear your energy fields and balance your chakras that I will share with you throughout the book.

The Chakras (Inner Energy Fields)

The base chakra (red in color), also called the *root chakra*, is located at the base of the spine and encompasses the spinal column, legs, feet, rectum, and immune system.

Diseases from imbalance of the base chakra include hemorrhoids, constipation, varicose veins, depression, attention deficit disorders, and immune-related disorders.

The sacral chakra (orange in color) is located in the lower abdomen, just below the navel. This is the area of emotional connection, creativity, manifestation, and releasing of old behavior patterns of the body.

Diseases from imbalance of the sacral chakra include gynecological and reproductive challenges, pelvic pain, urinary issues, and infections.

The solar plexus chakra (yellow in color) is located in the pit of the stomach and encompasses the stomach, upper abdomen, liver, rib cage, gall bladder, middle spine, spleen, kidneys, adrenals, and small intestines.

Diseases from imbalance of the solar plexus chakra include stomach ulcers, diabetes, indigestion, pancreatitis, hepatitis, arthritis, cirrhosis, and issues with self-esteem, self-image, fear of rejection, being unsure of oneself, willpower, confidence, and indecisiveness.

The heart chakra (green in color) is located at the center of the chest. The areas of the body affected are the heart, circulatory system, blood, lungs, diaphragm, breasts, shoulders, arms, hands, and esophagus.

Diseases from imbalance of the heart chakra include immunity disorders, heart and lung conditions, asthma, breast cancer, pneumonia, upper back and shoulder problems, and issues with self-love, self-confidence, jealousy, hate, fear, envy, and anger.

The throat chakra (blue in color) is located at the throat, in the neck region. The areas of the body influenced are the throat, thyroid, neck, mouth, teeth, gums, esophagus, and thyroid gland.

Diseases from imbalance of the throat chakra include sore throat, mouth ulcers, scoliosis, swollen glands, thyroid dysfunctions, laryngitis, tooth problems, TMJ, addiction, creativity blocks, and fear of making decisions.

The third-eye chakra (indigo in color) is located in the center of the brow. The areas of the body affected are the brain, neurological system, eyes, ears, nose, and pituitary and pineal glands.

Diseases from imbalance of the third-eye chakra include strokes, brain tumors, deafness, blindness, seizures, vertigo, learning disorders, depression, panic, spinal dysfunction, fear of the truth, and confusion.

The crown chakra (purple/violet in color) is located at the top of the head. The area of the body influenced is the top center of the head.

Diseases from imbalance of the crown chakra include issues with the skeletal system, muscular system, and skin; chronic fatigue syndrome; hypersensitivity to light, sound, and the environment; and lacking purpose, being uninspired, and being unable to view the full spectrum of life.

Auras (Outer Energy Fields)

If you are new to this information, know that auras are on the outside of the body and can change with your mood. The chakras are the energy centers inside your body that spin along the spine. Both energies are associated with color. The color of your chakras is consistent, but your aura colors change with your emotions in response to your life events. Anyone can see auras if they try to. Children are able to see the colors that surround you until our materialistic world's influence affects their sight.

There are numerous paintings of Jesus Christ and of the Buddha with golden halos painted around their heads. The painters of that time period could see the aura surrounding them and their natural golden light. As time has progressed and we have become a less spiritual people, we have lost this natural ability.

When I was in my early twenties, my then husband and I took our girls to the annual county fair in Michigan. There was a young girl with an easel set up on the sidewalk path to the fair. She was charging a small fee to draw your aura. She used large white poster paper and colored chalk. She looked at you and then quickly sketched a picture of the colors she saw protruding from your body. She drew all of the colors that she saw surrounding you. The colors were drawn as an arch or halo of color around you. This young girl had the ability to see the energy fields that surround any living thing. Over time I have come to understand that anyone can tune in and see the energy fields. You can see other people's energy fields with practice and good intentions. One way that you may begin to see auras is to relax and begin to see your own in the mirror. At first you will see a fuzziness or haziness around you, but with practice you will see color. A great time to try this exercise is after meditation. Through consistent meditation and pure intent, you will see the colors surrounding people. You will be able to see auras.

It is a true benefit to have the ability to tune into people's energy fields. You can see their true intent. Are they a good apple or a bad seed? Another great reason to see an aura is that you can see any dark or gray spots in the body that may be diseased. You can alert a person to have that area of the body checked out. Lives can be saved by this simple act.

Edgar Cayce, known as the most intuitive man of his time, was born in 1877 in Beverly, Kentucky, and died in 1945. He was called the "sleeping profit," as, while in a meditative state, he could answer any question asked of him regarding the past, the future, and health. Edgar Cayce is referenced as an American Christian Mystic. Cayce was a man of faith, who read the Bible once a year and taught Sunday school. Could you imagine being a kid in his class? He could see your aura and know by the colors whether you were a troublemaker and who you really were.

The last thing he wrote before he died was an essay on the auras and the meanings of the colors. The book is entitled *Auras: An Essay on the Meaning of Colors.* He wrote there, "The aura is the weathervane of the soul."[1] He believed that it is possible for everyone to see auras, and so do I. I've included for your reference this story from his last work, told to him by one of his friends:

> All during my childhood I saw colors in connection with people, but did not realize that it was uncommon. One day the appearance of a woman

in our neighborhood struck me as odd, though I could not for the moment see anything strange about her. When I got home I it suddenly struck me that she had no colors about her. Within a few weeks this woman died. That was my first experience with what I have learned to look upon as a natural action of nature.[2]

Cayce went on to say:

Apparently the aura reflects the vibrations of the soul. When a person is marked for death the soul begins to withdraw and the aura naturally fades. At the end there is only a slim connection and the break is easy. I have heard that when people died suddenly, in accidents, the passing was very difficult because the way had not been prepared.

A person's aura tells a great deal about him."[3]

Below are the colors associated with your energy fields and your aura, and their meanings. The aura can have many variations of the base colors, too many to count. Please note that when you meditate, you can visualize the color associated with each of the chakras. This will assist you in visibly seeing the colors. The colors gray or black can appear in a person's aura from disease or from dark negative energy.

Red is associated with energy, passion, strength, survival, courage, and warmth. In the aura, red can signify materialism, quick temper, anger, lack of forgiveness, obsessions, nervousness, and financial issues.

Orange is associated with relationship to the outside world and physical desires. Orange in your aura signifies creativity, thoughtfulness and kindness to others, and mastery in life.

Yellow is associated with intellect, happiness, power, and control. Yellow in your aura signifies communication, spiritual or material development, and one who is happy, friendly, and helpful.

Green is a symbol for love, truth, and compassion. A green aura signifies a professional healer or a natural healer.

Blue is associated with self-expression, truth, kindness, and communication. A blue aura signifies a spiritual or peace-loving person.

Indigo blue/purple is associated with intuition, inner wisdom, and clairvoyance. People with a purple aura are visionaries and are highly spiritual.

White is the perfect color we are all striving for. A white aura signifies a soul in perfect balance. Jesus has this aura.

I want to share with you what Edgar Cayce said about the healing power of colors and music:

Five hundred years before the birth of Christ, Pythagoras, the first philosopher, used colors for healing. Today medical science is just beginning to see the possibilities in this method. If colors are vibrations of the spiritual forces, they should be able to help in healing our deepest and most subtle maladies. Together with music, which is a kindred spiritual force, they form a great hope for the therapy of the future.[4]

Rosalyn L. Bruyere, international acclaimed healer and author of *Wheels of Light*, has this this to say about your aura and your chakras:

As we explore the aura and the Chakras, it is important for us to view our journey not as revolutionary, but rather as very traditional. Chakras, as well as auras and electromagnetic fields, are as old as the earth itself. The chakra system, in fact, is a part of the ancient and lost mysteries. And, in the end, the chakra system in our bodies is how we find our way back to the most ancient mystery of all—God, the Oneness, the Omniscient.[5]

Chapter 3

How to Clear Your Energy Fields

A SEA-SALT BATH is a quick and easy way to cleanse your chakras and clear your energy fields from unwanted debris. This works wonderfully when you come home from work or a crowded event, where you have been exposed to many people's energies. An overabundance of other people's energy may cause your chakras to become dim, depending on how well you protect yourself from other people's stuff.

All you need to do is run warm bathwater and sprinkle several tablespoonfuls of sea salt (found in groceries stores) evenly throughout the water (the more the better if it's your first time). Soak in the tub for at least twenty to thirty minutes. This is something that you should do often to stay balanced. The properties held within the salt will assist in balancing out your energy fields.

It is important that you do not use sea salt all of the time. Alternate your salt baths with a sugar scrub. Oftentimes sea salt is too harsh when used consistently; you may be adding salt to the wound, for example. Another great benefit to using a sugar scrub is that the sugar will make your energy field sweeter and people will act a bit kinder. Try this; the result is amazing! If you choose to make your own, here's a recipe for my favorite, an orange sugar scrub:

You will need:

½ cup + 2 tablespoons coconut oil

2 cups granulated sugar

6 drops orange essential oil

zest of one orange (grate the peel)

1–2 teaspoons ground cinnamon

Combine sugar and coconut oil in a small bowl. Mix until it becomes a paste. Add essential oil, orange zest, and ground cinnamon. Put into a jar and cover with the lid.

Another one of my favorite remedies for clearing any space is the steam of cinnamon. Yes, plain old powdered cinnamon, found in most households. Cinnamon has numerous benefits and healing properties: it is armed with antiviral, antibacterial, and antifungal properties. Cinnamon essential oils are used in aromatherapy in order to cleanse the air of airborne bacteria. When cinnamon oil is combined with another strong essential oil such as eucalyptus, tea tree, or rosemary oil, for example, the aroma kills 99 percent of the airborne bacteria circulating in the air.

Here is the recipe:

You will need:

A medium-sized saucepan filled with water

3-4 teaspoons ground cinnamon or

3 cinnamon sticks

Place the pot of water to boil on the stove. Add ground cinnamon or, even better, cinnamon sticks if you have them on hand. Bring to a boil. Lower the temperature, and let the steam seep out into the space.

The energy within the cinnamon is wonderful for clearing, as it can get into all the nooks and crannies of your home or workspace. It is the properties within the cinnamon steam that clear the air of negative energy. This is also a great thing to do during the holidays when the relatives are over. It is amazing how it changes the energy of the room.

Another helpful method to rid yourself of negative energy and balance your chakras is to exercise. Yoga, for example, is a wonderful way to keep your chakras balanced. I particularly like the exercises referenced in Peter Kelder's book, *Ancient Secret of the Fountain of Youth*. These exercises were acquired from his time spent in Tibet with the Tibetan monks, learning their ways. I mention these exercises because they have improved my upper-body strength and have kept me centered. The exercises take only about fifteen minutes to do daily. These particular exercises not only balance your chakras but help you strengthen essential muscles.

There are numerous meditations available to clear your chakras as well. This is a fun and easy way to stay clear. There are many awesome visualization CDs on the market today. Just pick up a CD, and follow along. I enjoy Doreen Virtue's book with audio download entitled *Chakra Clearing: Awakening Your Spiritual Power to Know and Heal*. It's powerful! I always feel rejuvenated when I complete the session with her.

Now here's something for you to think about: How many things do you touch with your hands on a daily basis? When you touch anything, you are intermingling with that object's energy and everyone else's energy who has used that object before you. As you go through your day, you may stop at the ATM machine. When you touch the keypad to enter your information, you are picking up the energy of all the other people who have used that ATM. When you are at the grocery store checkout counter and you enter your PIN number and accept the charge, you are again touching a heavily used keypad with an abundance of both good and bad energy. The next time you are at the keypad, before you punch in your number, take your hand and sweep it over the numbers and simply say, "Negative energy, begone!" or whatever you feel comfortable with. You are asking the Universe to remove any unwanted energies from the keypad so that they don't attach themselves to you and your card. The Universe will comply. Ask, and have pure intention.

Here is an effective exercise that I recommend if you have been exposed to unwanted energy often and want to clear yourself. This remedy comes from Rhonda, a spiritual colleague of mine. She instructs us to remove all of our jewelry from our hands. Next, you are to flick each finger with your other finger individually. As you are flicking each finger, you can actually feel the energy leaving your fingers—you are knocking off the energy. After flicking each finger, brush the energy off of you starting from your shoulder to your fingertips and send it up and out into the Universe to the light. When you do this, you actually feel the negative energy leaving your body. Try it! It's amazing to feel the unwanted energy leave your fingertips. Repeat the exercise for a couple of days or until you feel that the negative energy has been completely removed. Do not, however, repeat this exercise too often, as you will remove your positive energy, too. You can remove old negative energy from your legs, but you will need to have another person do this for you. What they will need to do is to start at the top of the leg and sweep the negative energy off each leg and the foot and send the energy into the light. Visualize the negative vibes ascending up into the white light above you. When you perform this exercise, you can feel a tingling sensation as the energy is coming off of your legs. The person working on you can feel it, too. Again, it is very important to clear yourself after removing someone else's negative energy from their body. You will take on their energy if you don't.

When your home or workplace feels negative, you can smudge it with a sage stick to remove the negativity from the space. Sage is one of the most powerful purifiers available. This is what the Native Americans use in New Mexico in their ceremonies to bless, cleanse, and heal a person or an object. The intention is to create a sacred space, using the smoke of the sage to get rid of any unwanted influences. When your intention is to remove any negative energy, you should use white sage if available. The healing properties contained within the sage smoke cleanse the negativity in your space. It is necessary for windows and a door to be open while you are smudging the room, as the old energy needs somewhere to go.

Light the sage stick, then fan the smoke throughout the space. Bless each room as you cleanse it. As you walk through each room, say, "Negative energy go, and positive energy stay. Bless my home/office," as the case may be. You can say different variations on this—whatever you feel comfortable with—but demand that the negative energy leave your space and that the positive energy remain. The room will feel lighter when you are finished.

You will find tiny crosses above all the doors in our home just to keep the negative energy out. You can do this simple act for protection. They're so small, no one knows they are there, but I do.

Salt, once a highly prized commodity, often goes unnoticed as a great energy neutralizer. This mineral has played a significant role in many religions and faiths. Salt has been used throughout history for purification, neutralizing negative energies, cleansing, and repelling negative vibrations. There are many references to salt in the Bible. In Christianity salt is a symbol of the sanctity of Jesus as a preserving value of his sanctity and protection. Salt has been used in the Roman Catholic Church to make holy water and for protective circles in exorcisms. Salt is considered to be a very favorable substance in Hinduism and is used in certain religious ceremonies. The most important fact that I have learned about salt is that it absorbs the negative energy. You can place a bowl of sea salt in a room in your home, and the salt will neutralize the energy of the room as it absorbs the negative vibes.

If you are concerned about negative people entering into or around your home, you can sprinkle salt outside your front door as the Hawaiians do. If you want to be thorough, you should sprinkle salt around the perimeter of the entire home/property. This will deter any negative people from crossing the threshold. It is amazing to watch this in action. I have placed salt across the threshold of my door before an event (as a regular practice) and watched in amazement as certain people were unable to enter. It looks as if there is an invisible shield blocking them as they try to walk through the front door. It appears comical, but is amazing how energy works.

As a young, single mom with two little girls, I often felt uncomfortable and afraid and began to ask God for help. I imagined that we were protected within a bubble of heavenly white light. I don't remember who taught me how to do this or whether I just knew intuitively to visualize the three of us surrounded by white light and say, "God, please surround me and my children with your heavenly light so that no harm comes to us." I did not carry a weapon, so this is what I relied on to protect us. We always remained safe. It was interesting to observe what happened after I would do this. People would never bother us; it was as if we were invisible or something. Over the years I have learned to surround myself with a white net of light, realizing that I was blocking all energy from myself with the bubble. Try visualizing a fisherman's net with either gold or white light cloaked over you. This still allows the good energy to come through.

I surround myself with light for protection when traveling and when encountering a large crowd of people. I may do this when I am in a place where the energy just does not feel good, where I can physically feel negative energy around me. We all have this ability, and it takes but just a moment to do. I have to confess that every time I have forgotten to shield myself, I get some negative, nasty person trying to get into my bubble (or my energy field).

This next exercise I want to share with you is to remove energy blockages. This occurs often when you are on the wrong path in life and the energy is not flowing through your body properly. I was having a terrible pain in the left side of my chest and phoned my friend who is a fellow spiritual worker to ask her opinion. She suggested that I write down on a piece of paper that I would like to remove any negative blockages or unbalanced energies that do not belong in my body and that may be preventing my progress in life. After doing this exercise, my pain was completely gone.

Here are the words I have been taught to use:

From myself I burn away all adverse blockages, unbalanced energies, negative entities, that which does not belong, that which impedes my progress, that which impedes my prosperity, that which impedes my good health, and send them into the light to be healed and resolved as I am healed from them. Restore my divine peace, protection, good health and prosperity, and the divine flow of balanced energy on all levels. So it is. Thank you.[6]

Send this negativity into the heavenly light, and ask to be healed and restored to divine peace. Burn the piece of paper completely. The negativity will be gone after the paper is burned. I always sign my name to the paper to make it stick. You may think this is an odd thing to do, but the power of your words, along with the intention you give it, makes it stick. These words hold much power and will accomplish your goal.

Chapter 4

Release the Old Energy
with Massage and Music

Massage Therapy

Another way to remove the old energy that gets in our muscles and bones is with massage. Having a massage will do wonders for your body, mind, and spirit. I believe that having a massage once a month should be mandatory for all human beings. When we get stressed out, our muscles tend to tense up. Our whole body is full of stressed-out energy. You may say, I'm not that stressed out, I don't need a massage. You would be surprised that most often you do. We are souls living in these shells called bodies, and we need to keep our energy flowing. Stress in the body with no release causes blockages in your energy fields. We all experience a certain level of stress in our lives every day whether we ask for it or not. Having a massage releases a lot of that stored-up old energy that gets in your bones, muscles, and tissue.

Releasing this energy releases the stress and negativity. As a result you are a more relaxed and happy soul when your massage is complete.

I am usually a little lightheaded when I leave my massage, as the body needs to rebalance itself. The massage therapist will instruct you to drink plenty of water after a massage. This will prevent you from feeling dizzy. The lightheadedness comes from the release of toxic energy from your body.

I am often concerned about where the negative energy has gone. My hope is that all experienced massage therapists know how to clear themselves. Please be careful if you are massaging a friend or a partner: you don't want to take on all their stuff, their energy. Make sure you clear yourself after you massage someone.

Here's a funny story: After having a stressful day, my husband came home from work with negative energy attached to him. I was so anxious to give him a massage to release his stress that I did not protect myself. I took on all of his stuff. As a result I became cranky and irritable. He was fine, happy-go-lucky. We both laughed when we realized what had happened. It was apparent that I took on his negative energy. This has happened to me more than once as I just wasn't paying enough attention. I am more aware of how the Universal Energy operates and make sure I protect my energy field. You need to be able to clear yourself of any negative energy that you may have taken on while working on someone. Visualize protection around yourself before you give a massage, and take a sea-salt bath in the evening to clear your energy before bed. If you are like most people, you will be sore after getting a massage, but after a day or two, you will feel like a new person. It's as if you have been cleansed.

I want to add that when you book your session, there are different types of massages for various ailments that may be offered. Consider your options before booking your appointment. You may want a sports massage if you work out often, or something more subtle and soothing to relax. Many spas have wonderful couple's massages that are fun. The bottom line is you need to do this for yourself. Having a massage on a regular basis will help balance your mental and physical well-being. It will also help your relationship if you both get massages on a regular basis. You are just a better person after the old energy is released from your body.

Music Energy

Another way that people's energy fields are healed is by the vibrations of music. It is amazing how the vibrations of music can change your mood. Think about how happy you are when you are driving down the road, listening to your favorite song with the volume cranked up. You have changed your emotional state. On the other side of the spectrum, a melancholy tone can convey the feeling of sadness. Music is uplifting to the soul and soothing to the heart! The vibrations of musical instruments and song have an energetic effect on our souls, the harp in particular.

Harp

When music is played on the harp, the vibrations of the harp strings go into the body and balance an ill person's frequencies. Carrol McLaughlin, an award-winning professor and healer, is in charge of one of the largest harp departments in the world. The renowned concert harpist explains that when someone has an area of weakness in their body, it means that it's not vibrating at its full frequency. She conducted a healing experiment at a hospital's ICU unit. She played her harp for a number of patients. The result was a 27 percent reduction in pain without any change in their medications. It has been documented that she played for a man in a coma and that after seven minutes he took off his breathing mask and said, "Thank you."[7] Another patient was ready to go into hospice, but after the patient heard Carrol play her music, the doctor canceled the hospice plans because the patient's vital signs had improved dramatically.[8] We should all have a harp that we can play to keep us healthy and vibrant!

An International Harp Therapy Program that trains and certifies its practitioners to heal with the harp is established today.[9] Now that's amazing! This demonstrates the miraculous healing that occurs when your energy fields are out of balance. Music is healing to the soul for all of us. I know that when I listen to an upbeat song on the radio, it makes me feel energized and happy. The vibrations of music have been healing us for centuries and continue to do so today. Did you know the harp is mentioned in the Bible sixty-six times?

Sing joyfully to the LORD, you righteous;
it is fitting for the upright to praise him.
Praise the LORD with the harp;
make music to him on the ten-stringed lyre.

Sing him a new song;
play skillfully, and shout for joy.

For the word of the LORD is right and true;
he is faithful in all he does.
The LORD loves righteousness and justice;
the earth is full of his unfailing love.

—Psalm 33:1–5

Tibetan singing bowls

These "singing bowls," as they are called, are another fascinating way to balance your energy fields. They date back to the time of Buddha Shakyamuni (560–480 BC).

In Buddhist tradition, the singing bowls, also known as the "Himalayan bowls," are used in yoga, sound healing, religious ceremonies, and music therapy. They bring about the energy of tranquility and peacefulness to the soul. Traditionally, a singing bowl signals the beginning and the end of silent meditation cycles. The bowls bring about a deep state of relaxation to our bodies by creating a range of sounds to restore the natural vibrating frequency. If the body is diseased and out of harmony, it is balanced by the vibrations emanating from the bowl. Even if you cannot hear the sounds, the vibrations of the bowl and the frequency still resonate into the body and balance your energy fields.

That is why you will find singing bowls in meditation centers, monasteries, and temples throughout the world. Singing bowls are often referred to as a type of bell, as the tone is produced by tapping the side of the metal bowl with a rubber mallet, then rubbing the mallet clockwise around the outside edge of the rim of the bowl, causing the rim to vibrate to produce the sound. The ancient Tibetan bowls produced harmonic overtones, emitting a beautiful vibrating tone. I feel that they are extremely therapeutic to the mind, body, and soul. Many professionals, among them medical doctors, chiropractors, energy workers, massage and bodywork practitioners, meditation teachers, ministers, musicians, psychologists, singers, Reiki practitioners, voice coaches, and yoga instructors, use the singing bowls for healing.

Mitchell Gaynor, MD, former director of Medical Oncology and Integrated Medicine at the Cornell Cancer Prevention Center in New York, was one of the pioneers in this type of therapy. He used sound, chanting, and music in conjunction with metal and crystal bowls as an addition to conventional treatment of cancer patients. Dr. Gaynor is also a best-selling author, having published numerous books, including *The Healing Power of Sound: Recovery from Life-Threatening Illness Using Sound, Voice, and Music*. This is what Dr. Gaynor said regarding how we are healed in this manner:

> If we accept that sound is vibration and we know that vibration touches every part of our physical being, then we understand that sound is heard not only through the ears but through every cell in our bodies. One reason sound heals on a physical level is because it so deeply touches and transforms us on the emotional and spiritual planes. Sound can redress imbalances on every level of physiologic

functioning and can play a positive role in the treatment of virtually any medical disorder.[10]

Crystal bowls

The use of crystal bowls in healing intrigues me as much as, or more than, the use of the metal Tibetan bowls. I believe that the crystal bowls hold much healing power because of the combination of sound healing, crystal healing, and color healing within them. These bowls are made of various precious stones. You can acquire different sizes of bowls and choices of stones depending upon your intention. There are singing bowls carved of amethyst, rose quartz, aquamarine, garnet, citrine, and emerald; the options are extensive. Each of the stones has its own unique healing energy.

Elivia Melodey is a renowned sound healer who uses the crystal bowls for healing. She says:

> When the sound moves through the atmosphere and touches us, it causes our cells to move in different directions at a different speed, in rhythm with the sound wave. This puts us in harmony with the sound wave, the world and ourselves. The sound penetrates into our very cells and rebalances them through oscillation and resonance.[11]

Om

I cannot complete this chapter without addressing the sound of *Om* (*Aum*). This is often the first and the last sound you hear at a yoga class. Many have described *Om* as the vibration of the Universe. If you have never experienced the vibration of *Om*, or even if you have, try it now! To pronounce *Om* properly, the sound vibration is pronounced "oom," like "home" with a Midwestern accent. When you pronounce *Om*, it resonates through your body and your soul. Try it. It's kind of freaky, as you're not expecting this intense vibration that seems to hum inside your body. When you say this mantra, you can actually feel the balancing of your energy fields.

Tones and Chakras

I could write an entire book on the healing energy of music and its many facets. The vibrations of the tones continue to bring joy to all of us. Music in its many forms has healed our souls from the beginning of time and continues to lend its energy of harmony to our world. Edgar Cayce said in his last essay, "If colors are vibrations of spiritual forces, they should be able to help in healing our deepest and most subtle maladies. Together with music, which is a kindred spiritual force, they form a great hope for therapy of the future."[12]

Cayce wrote that the following are the musical tones that heal each chakra:

Base chakra: do

Root chakra: re

Solar plexus chakra: mi

Heart chakra: fa

Throat chakra: sol

Third-eye chakra: la

Crown chakra: ti[13]

> *If you want to find the secrets of the Universe,*
> *think in terms of energy, frequency and vibration.*
> —Nikola Tesla

Chapter 5

The Healing and Spiritual
Energy of Essential Oils

I CAN STILL RECALL walking into the dimly lit room for a massage and becoming acutely aware of a pleasant, almost calming odor in the air. It smelled so foreign to me: What was this fragrance? The aroma made me feel happy and relaxed all at the same time. There were several small machines throughout the spa, shooting a beautiful-smelling mist up and out into the air. You just couldn't quite put your finger on what it was, but you knew the aroma was rich and uplifting. I have come to know these scents as eucalyptus, lavender, frankincense, myrrh, sandalwood, and many more. The health benefits of applying and inhaling these precious oils are priceless for our health and well-being.

Aromatherapy has become more popular today than ever, as science has found that pure, therapeutic-grade essential oils have enormous benefits to our health. As I began to learn about the essential oils, I realized there is a huge community of people who are just as fascinated by their healing properties as I am. People in the United States, as well as across the globe, are getting back to basics and using the oils to heal themselves. These oils are not just used as aromatherapy, they are also used topically when diluted. I began researching and working with these healing oils and came to realize that they dated back to biblical times. The oils are mentioned more than two hundred times in the New and Old Testaments of the Bible. There are actually twelve essential oils mentioned in the Bible: calamus, cinnamon, frankincense, juniper, cassia, cypress, galbanum, myrrh, cedar wood, fir, hyssop, and myrtle.

As children many of us are taught the Bible story of the three wise men. They brought the baby Jesus the gifts of frankincense and myrrh, as these oils were very precious in those times. The baby Jesus was anointed with spikenard, a spiritual oil used for relaxing, centering, and grounding the body. It is used for conditions of the heart and the nervous system today. I did not realize how precious these oils were. They were more expensive than gold in biblical times because the people knew that they held healing properties within them. Essential oils were used in ancient times for anointing and cleansing, in medicines and ointments, and for aromatic healing, and each oil holds a special energy within it to cure our ailments. This is what the oils were intended for.

After researching the compounds of the oils and what they were used for, I learned that the oils penetrate our skin rather quickly. As I studied further, I was reminded that in biblical times, the oils were applied to people's feet. I discovered this was done because the pores of the feet are large and can absorb the oils more easily and quickly. Once absorbed into the body, the oils can last up to a week. Now that's amazing healing power!

Oils each have their own unique frequency, and each part of the body has a frequency as well. Research has shown that the frequency of an oil causes it to be attracted to the like frequency within the body. The quickest way to absorb the oils is through the inhalation of the mist. The second quickest way is through the feet, then the ears.

One of the most important oils to keep on hand is called "thieves' oil." This story explains the reason why. During the Black Death plague of the sixteenth century, a band of thieves was apprehended and brought before the king. The king forced them to explain how they were able to steal money and jewelry from the deceased victims and not contract the highly contagious disease themselves. The king, of course, wanted to protect his family and his kingdom from getting the plague as well. The thieves confessed that they came from a family of apothecaries. With their knowledge of healing remedies passed down through generations, they were able to combine specific oils extracted from plants. With the right combination of oils, they could protect themselves from the plague. This historic occurrence shows the power within the essential oils and the healing power they provide for us as God intended.

The recipe for thieves' oil can still be found in the Royal English Archives to this day. The recipe includes clove, lemon, cinnamon, rosemary, and eucalyptus. This combination of oils in the Thieves® proprietary blend was tested at Weber State University in Ogden, Utah. The findings show a 99.96 percent effective rate against airborne bacteria.[14] We are fortunate that thieves' oil is sold today by many vendors across the country. We use thieves' oil in our household for cleaning and disinfecting. Essential oil companies have created cleaning solutions, dish soap, dishwasher soap, and hand soap using the thieves' oil blend.

All of the essential oils are unique, but frankincense has become one of my favorite essential oils for its favorable aroma and its wealth of healing properties. During biblical times this oil was more highly valued than gold. My research has led me to purchase 100 percent pure frankincense oil from the *Boswellia sacra* tree. I have not been disappointed. Frankincense is tapped from these trees by stripping the bark and extracting the resin to be used in various ways. The oil comes from the Arabian Peninsula and North Africa, principally Oman, Yemen, and Somalia. Frankincense, known for its healing powers since the time of Christ, helps with allergies, insect bites, bronchitis, cancer, respiratory infections, diphtheria, headaches, hemorrhaging, herpes, high blood pressure, inflammation, stress, tonsillitis, typhoid, and warts. Many people use frankincense oil in aromatherapy to clear their house or office of unwanted energies.

Frankincense has been used for centuries as a folk medicine because of its anti-inflammatory properties. This precious oil is used today as incense, in perfume, for treating asthma, gastroenteritis, skin conditions, and more. It is also used for emotional balance and improving the immune system, the nervous system, and the skin and nails. Frankincense has a composition of 8 percent sesquiterpenes and 78 percent monoterpenes. The compound has been effective in treating Alzheimer's disease, Lou Gehrig's disease, Parkinson's disease, and multiple sclerosis. It is proven to be mood elevating and oxygenating and is said to deprogram miswritten or messed-up DNA code, which I find fascinating. The Lord gave us all of these natural tools to heal ourselves. I believe it's time we get back to the basics and use the oils as they were intended.

Recent research shows that a chemical compound in the resin of frankincense demonstrates the ability to fight cancer in late-stage ovarian cancer cells. In 2013, Leicester University researchers announced findings that AKBA (acetyl-11-keto-beta-boswellic acid), a chemical compound in the resin, has cancer-killing properties and has the potential to destroy ovarian cancer cells.[15]

A few years ago the BBC reported from Salalah, Oman, where immunologist Dr. Mahmoud Suhail was working on the cancer-fighting properties of the ancient resin. He said:

> [Some types of c]ancer start[] when the DNA code within the cell's nucleus becomes corrupted. It seems frankincense has a re-set function. It can tell the cell what the right DNA code should be.
>
> Frankincense separates the 'brain' of the cancerous cell—the nucleus—from the 'body'—the

cytoplasm, and closes down the nucleus to stop it
reproducing corrupted DNA codes.[16]

Now that is amazing! No wonder the three wise men
brought this precious oil with its many healing properties as
a gift to the Messiah.

When God created us, He created many trees and plants
to heal us. My essential oil research led me back to the early
beginnings. The first recipe for anointing oil is found in the
book of Exodus.

> *Then the Lord said to Moses, "Take the following fine spices: 500*
> *shekels of liquid myrrh, half as much (that is, 250 shekels) of fragrant*
> *cinnamon, 250 shekels of fragrant calamus, 500 shekels of cassia—all*
> *according to the sanctuary shekel—and a hin of olive oil. Make these*
> *into a sacred anointing oil, a fragrant blend, the work of a perfumer. It*
> *will be a sacred anointing oil. Then use it anoint the tent of meeting,*
> *the ark of the covenant law, the table and all its articles, the lamp stand*
> *and its accessories, the altar of incense, the altar of burnt offering and*
> *all its utensils, and the basin with its stand. You shall consecrate them*
> *so they will be most holy, and whatever touches them will be holy."*
>
> —Exodus 30:22–29

It's intriguing to realize that we have had these natural
healing oils since the very beginning of time. (As a side note:
500 shekels equals approximately 12½ pounds; a *hin* equals
approximately 1 gallon.) I was very excited to mix these oils
together—until I continued reading further:

"'Do not pour it on anyone else's body and do not make any other oil using the same formula. It is sacred, and you are to consider it sacred.'"

—Exodus 30:32

After much thought and deliberation, I concluded that the Old Testament recipe was written so that we may realize the immense healing properties that the oils hold. God wanted us to use this knowledge for our benefit. I believe things changed when Jesus came into the picture. Not only did He use anointing oil, but He sent His disciples out and instructed them to do the same.

It is a good idea to keep a bottle of 100 percent pure lavender essential oil in your home. This oil is a natural antibiotic, antiseptic, sedative, and antidepressant. It is very effective on burns and is known to prevent scarring. Lavender oil will stimulate the immune system contributing to the healing process. This herb is also wonderful for insomnia, anxiety, depression, and fatigue. Treat yourself next time you take a bath and add ten to twelve drops of lavender essential oil to your bathwater to relax. Even better, place lavender oil in your aromatic infuser to relax, as research at the University of Maryland Medical Center has confirmed that lavender produces slight calming, soothing, and sedative effects when its scent is inhaled. Scientific evidence suggests that aromatherapy with lavender may slow the activity of the nervous system, improve sleep quality, promote relaxation, and lift the mood in people suffering from sleep disorders. Studies also suggest that massage with lavender essential oil results in improved sleep quality, a more stable mood, better concentration, and reduced anxiety for people.[17]

They went out and preached that people should repent. They drove out many demons and anointed many sick people with oil and healed them.

—Mark 6:12-13

In recent years research has been conducted to measure the electrical frequency of the precious oils in megahertz (MHz). The results have shown essential oils to have electrical frequencies of 52 MHz to 320 MHz. This is amazingly high, considering that the human body was measured with the same device at 62 MHz to 68 MHz. The developer of the equipment is Bruce Tainio of Tainio Technology in Cheney, Washington, and D. Gary Young, an expert on essential oils. They worked together to evaluate the oils to come up with these findings.

After working with the oils, I am surprised at how they have become a part of our daily lives. The oils can change your energy for the better. My aromatic diffuser runs constantly at home, infused with the essential oil best suited for the day. Some of my favorite oils to use in our home are lavender, frankincense, myrrh, cinnamon, sandalwood, clary sage, peppermint, and lemon. The citrus oils, like lemon, grapefruit, and orange, are uplifting to our energy fields.

Another oil used by many people every day is tea tree oil, another magnificent oil with many uses. The Australian Aborigines have used the oil of the indigenous tea tree for centuries as an antiseptic for skin conditions. They also used the tree leaves for medications. The oil is used today for problem skin, as a scalp treatment, and for pest control. Tea tree oil is in many of our cleaning products, and people add the oil to their laundry daily. It is beneficial in so many ways because of its antiviral, antibacterial, and antifungal properties. I add several drops in with the detergent, and the clothes come out smelling fresh and clean and the negative energy is washed away.

Essential oils hold an extremely high electrical energy, which is why they are so powerful in cleaning and for healing. The Lord has given us these oils to use to keep us healthy and vibrant. I believe that essential oils are a rediscovered blessing to all who use them. My hope is that more and more people will become enlightened and make essential oils a part of their everyday life.

I love what Valerie Ann Worwood, author of *The Complete Book of Essential Oils and Aromatherapy*, has to say regarding the oils:

> *Essential oils are one of the great untapped resources of the world. Here we have a system of natural help that is far more than a system of medicine that can prevent illness and alleviate symptoms. These extremely complex liquids are extracted from very specific species of plant life and are in harmony with people and planet alike.*[18]

47

Chapter 6

The Energy of Water

WHEN I AM CLOSE to a body of water, I feel calmer and more relaxed. I feel a sense of peace within my soul. The energy of the water is calming to us. I am sure many of you have experienced the same feeling. My belief is that since the average human body is made up of 55–75 percent water, we are just naturally drawn to it. It makes sense that we feel balanced and at peace when in or by the water. We all enjoy a trip to the ocean to hear the soothing sound of the waves crashing against the shore. The sound of the waves and the smell of the fresh ocean air make me sleep like a baby.

Because of my love for water, I have become a huge fan of the Jacuzzi tub, mineral baths, and just taking baths in general. I jump in our hot tub or the bathtub whenever I have the opportunity. When you are in the bath, you tend to completely relax and that's nice! Jacuzzi tubs are wonderful for relaxation and therapeutic for your joints and muscles. You can greatly benefit from this form of relaxation. The energy of the hot circulating mineral water is therapeutic for the body and the soul.

Ancient legend has credited the early Celtic kings with the discovery of hot springs in Bath, England. Many cultures throughout the world, such as the Native Americans, Persians, Babylonians, Egyptians, Greeks, and Romans, have used, and still have a strong belief in, the therapeutic and spiritual purification of mineral baths.

The Dead Sea, known in the Bible as the "Salt Sea," has the capability to rehabilitate and restore physiological functions. People flock to the lowest spot on the face of the earth to enjoy this natural health spa. Because of its salinity, there exist no life forms of any kind. The Dead Sea is nearly ten times more salty than the world's oceans, containing 340 grams of salt per liter of water. People go to this spiritual place to put the black mud on their bodies. The mud is full of Dead Sea minerals and organic elements from the shoreline. This mineral mud improves and stimulates blood circulation throughout the body. This black mud also helps many types of joint disease and softens the skin. The Dead Sea and its energy is here for our use, as God intended us to relax and rejuvenate our bodies.

One of the best things you can do for your body is to stay hydrated with H_2O. Trust me, your kidneys will thank you. Yes, your kidneys. The kidneys remove waste products and excess fluid from the body. The kidneys' function is so important that the Lord gave you two of them to flush all of those impurities and bad energy out of your body daily. Water is an excellent and natural detoxifier. Your kidneys regulate the amount of potassium, salt, and acid that is in the body. Given this fact, there is always the question of how much water we require each day. According to the Institute of Medicine, an adequate intake for men is approximately 13 cups of water (3 liters) per day. For women, a good intake of water is 9 cups (2.2 liters) each day.[19] Staying hydrated relieves fatigue and improves your mood. Research has shown that mild dehydration can negatively affect clear thinking and alter your mood.

The benefits of drinking alkaline water have come to my attention for its many healthful properties. It is known to boost the immune system, promote better digestion, improve energy levels, slow the aging process, enhance your complexion, and assist with weight loss. What is alkaline water? It is water that has been separated into alkaline and acid fractions using electrolysis, which takes advantage of the naturally occurring electrical charges found in the magnesium and calcium ions in the drinking water. They say that alkaline water is less acidic than tap water. The term *alkaline* refers to the water's pH level. You can purchase alkaline bottled water, or you can make your own. There are companies selling ionizers that the manufactures say have the ability to make regular tap water alkaline through the chemical process of electrolysis. The creators of the ionizers explain that electricity is used to separate molecules in the water to make it more acidic or more alkaline. There are also many countertop pitchers that you can find online and in stores that filter water and turn it alkaline. Here is a recipe to make alkaline water by adding one of the following ingredients: baking soda, which is highly alkaline; lemons, which are anionic, so that when your body digests the lemon water you drink, it reacts with the anionic properties of the lemon, making the water alkaline; or pH drops, which are manufactured to add a specified level of alkalinity.

You will need:

8-ounce glass of water

⅛ tablespoon baking soda *or*

juice of 1 lemon *or*

pH drops (amount according to manufacturer's directions)

Add one of the alkalizing agents to the water and drink!

Lemon water has been my drink of choice for many years. I must have realized the benefits intuitively. Unfortunately, not enough data has been gathered to date to prove the effectiveness of alkaline water, but the energetic concept makes complete sense to me.

You may have heard of a gentleman by the name of Masaru Emoto, who studied water and the energy that it holds. Emoto was born in Japan in 1943 and just recently died, in 2014. He was an author with a *New York Times* bestseller. He published volumes of work called *Messages from Water*. In his works are pictures of ice crystals and his experiments with them. He claimed that human consciousness has an effect on the molecular structure of water. Emoto believed that the energy and the vibrations of water change the physical structure of this precious liquid. He also believed that water is the blueprint of our reality.[20]

His experiments consisted of exposing water in glasses to various words, music, and pictures. He then froze the water and examined the crystals with microscopic photography. He claimed that water exposed to positive speech and thought would result in beautifully formed frozen crystals and that negative intentions produced ugly crystals. He also studied water from a mountain stream. The water, when frozen, showed structures of beautifully shaped geometric designs, yet the polluted water he used in his experiment produced crystal structures that were distorted and randomly formed. Emoto believed he could change polluted water by exposing it to ultraviolet light and certain electromagnetic waves.[21] When you understand the power of energy, you realize that he may have been on to something.

Now that you know about the energy of water, I want to mention that getting a mineral bath is therapeutic for the body and soul. I am fortunate to have visited many wonderful mineral baths in Colorado and New Mexico. One of my favorite spots to take a mineral bath is in Jemez Springs, New Mexico. The little town of Jemez Springs has wonderful natural hot springs with mineral baths, wraps, and massages at various establishments. The minerals help to get rid of the negative toxins in our bodies. It's a wonderful natural cleansing process, as well as a great way to really pamper yourself and relax. Some of the mineral baths are indoors, and some are outdoors along the Jemez River. It's an invigorating experience and very therapeutic. Check and see if there are any hot springs in your area. It will be worth your time: the energy of water is soothing to the body and rejuvenating to the soul.

Chapter 7

The Power of Prayer

IT IS IMPORTANT THAT I address the power of prayer. Many people do not realize what powerful energy prayer holds. When you believe in the Universe and its energy, you start to realize that nothing is accidental. God our Creator orchestrated the energy to work for our benefit. Prayer is part of the energy we can tap into to better our lives and the lives of others. Prayer is written about in the Bible numerous times. The concept of prayer should make sense to you, for as we have learned thus far, the energy of your words and your intention is extremely powerful.

Now that you understand this concept, imagine how a group of people praying for the same results can create miracles. That is why when a large group of people pray for the same outcome, the results are often favorable. Miracles are created. Imagine the energy of many people focused on the same result. The energy is magnified.

When Jesus spoke to the masses, He told them to ask for anything in His name:

"Ask and it will be given to you; seek and you will find; knock and the door will be opened to you. For everyone who asks receives; the one who seeks finds; and to the one who knocks, the door will be opened.

"Which of you, if your son asks for bread, will give him a stone? Or if he asks for a fish, will give him a snake? If you, then, though you are evil, know how to give good gifts to your children, how much more will your Father in heaven give good gifts to those who ask him! So in everything, do to others what you would have them do to you, for this sums up the Law and the Prophets."

—Matthew 7:7–12

He was teaching us spiritual law. This concept makes a lot of sense. The following is a passage from the Bible reiterating his teachings:

"Therefore I tell you, whatever you ask in prayer, believe that you have received it, and it will be yours."

—Mark 11:24

Prayer is answered only by God with His divine power. When you are praying for something, believe that your prayer is already answered. It is imperative that you have faith that your prayer will be answered. After you pray for what you desire, let it go. Let the energy go out into the Universe for God to answer; do not dwell on the outcome. This is the same concept as saying positive affirmations. You are directing the energy to achieve the intended result. Have faith that the Lord will answer your prayer with what you requested or something even better. This is reiterated in the book of James:

> *But when you ask, you must believe and not doubt, because the one who doubts is like a wave of the sea, blown and tossed by the wind. That person should not expect to receive anything from the Lord. Such a person is double-minded and unstable in all they do.*
>
> —James 1:6–8

Remember, our Creator gives us only what is good for us. You may pray for a better position with your present employer, only to receive an even better job with an increase in pay at a new company. God knows what is best for us even when we don't. When you begin to pay attention to this concept, you will recognize a pattern.

I have witnessed many times how prayer can help with relationship issues. You may be in a relationship that is not working out for you and you pray for the situation to get better. If the relationship is the best thing for both parties involved, it will work out. If it's not, God will send the right person to you—the one who is perfect for you. In the past I have prayed for a relationship to work out, but it did not. Now I am glad that my prayers were not answered. God made sure I met the right person for me, and my relationship is better than I could have ever imagined it to be. God knew what was best for me even when I did not. It is up to you to recognize this. Your prayers will always be answered, but the answer may not be what you were expecting. When prayer is sincere and comes from within your heart, you should expect miracles. Pray for one another often. Your prayers will make a difference. I love these words from Tenzin Gyatso, the fourteenth Dalai Lama:

> I have found that the greatest degree of inner tranquility comes from the development of love and compassion.
>
> The more we care for the happiness of others, the greater our own sense of well-being. Cultivating a close, warmhearted feeling for others automatically puts the mind at ease. It is the ultimate source of success in life.[22]

The more you pray and the more compassion you have for others, the more blessed you will become.

Duke University doctors have studied nontraditional influences on healing. They took twenty heart patients and put them in a prayer group. The patients were not aware that their names had been placed on a prayer list. The list was sent to Nepal, Jerusalem, and Baltimore, where people of all different faiths prayed for their recovery. Doctors say that the patients who were in the prayer group performed fifty to one hundred times better than the people who were not prayed for.[23]

I do believe in the power of prayer, but I also believe we all have a destiny to fulfill. Throughout these pages you will learn from my story how my prayers were answered. You will discover my struggle to have faith in God and how I learned to work with the Universal Energy.

When I began to pray again, it was because I was at a point in my life where I did not know what else to do. I was taught to pray as a child, but that time seemed so long ago. I was in an unhappy marriage, with two small children. I wondered how I had gotten myself and them into such a mess. Here I was in my late twenties and on my second marriage. My second husband was a very handsome, charismatic man, but I learned quickly that these qualities were not the ingredients for a good match. I was a pretty girl and thought at the time that looks, charm, and personality were the most important qualities in a man. It took me many years to find out differently. I had no idea my husband was a verbally abusive person when I married him. He was constantly yelling at me and the kids. Crystal was nine, and Samantha was four. Poor Crystal used to shudder when he screamed at her. Her stepfather was not a cruel person; he just did not know how to handle little children or any type of stress. His father had died when he was a young man, so he really had no fatherly example to learn from. Early on in our marriage I realized he was not able to hold a job for any length of time, either. So I became the breadwinner. I did not mind working. My father was a very hard worker, and I inherited his work ethic by example. I think it's in your blood. I wanted this marriage to be a partnership where we both worked hard and had the same goals for our family. I hoped for a nice life for us.

I was managing a retail store in Michigan at that time. As the store manager I was required to work many nights and weekends. I enjoyed being successful at my job. My position gave me confidence, and I did fairly well financially. I enjoyed my work and was happy to be able to provide for us. The drawback was that I was away from the children most of the time. As a result, the influence that my husband and the babysitters were having on them was not what I had hoped for.

On the day I knelt down to pray, I was at my wits' end. I had not prayed in a very long time. I asked God for guidance: "What should I do about my situation?" I was very unhappy and asked God to please help me. I know that many people wait until something tragic happens in their lives to pray to God, and at this time, I was one of them. I had reached my breaking point with my marital situation and was desperate for help. As I was finishing my prayer, I heard the mailbox outside the window shut. We had one of those mailboxes that attach to the house by the front door. I got up from my knees and opened the door. I took the letters out of the box. There were so many letters from the bank, I wondered what all of this was about. All of the checks that I had written for our household bills had been returned unpaid. I began to panic: What had happened? I had deposited my paycheck in the bank, and I knew I had not been that far off in my calculations. I jumped in the car and drove straight to our local bank.

I anxiously waited to speak to the banker to find out what had happened to our checking account. She was very nice and businesslike as she looked over our account. Her eyes looked sad as she shook her head and showed me the large withdrawal that had been made a few days earlier by my husband.

The banker looked at me with a sorrowful look on her face and asked, "Does your husband have a gambling problem?"

I just stared at her for a moment while I processed what she was asking me. I was stunned. It was as if a light switched on in my brain and I realized that my husband had screwed up again. He must have owed somebody money or loaned a friend money without my knowledge. Who knew what it was this time? He had made mistakes in the past but never to this extreme. My husband was not able to handle money. This time he had gone too far. We had two small children to care for. The checks that had been returned were for our utility bills, our house payment, and our car payment.

I recall that rainy morning like it was yesterday. I drove home in a daze. By the time I reached my house, I was angry. I worked so hard for my money. This was not what I had signed up for when I got married. Maybe I was too naive to realize what I had signed up for. I just could not fathom this: How could he do this to our family? I knew I had to do something, but what? I did not have any family in Michigan any longer. My parents had relocated to New Mexico for my father's job a few years earlier. My sisters lived in Ohio and Florida. I was on my own. All I could think of was that God had answered my prayers. He showed me what I needed to see. I want to mention to be careful what you ask for when you pray; you may just receive your answer. Sometimes the answer is not what you thought it would be. All I knew at this point was that I had to get myself and my children out of this situation. And I was determined to do it!

My parents were not too fond of my second husband. As a silent protest they did not attend our wedding. I could not very easily call them and tell them that my second marriage was not working and that my husband had drained our bank account. I just wasn't up for the "I told you so" routine. I was not up for that negativity at this point in my life. I was a hard-working girl and did my best to be a good wife to my husband and a great mom to the girls. I tried to remain as positive as I could under these circumstances, although it was difficult.

Now, when these things happen in life, God always seems to hand you an unexpected blessing. I was fortunate to have met a very nice lady at this time. Her name was Naomi. I look back now and realize that to meet her was part of God's plan for me. We had met at a psychic party. I cannot even tell you who held the party or why I went. Naomi read my tarot cards and seemed to realize I was not in a good situation. She said there was light at the end of the tunnel for me. That part was comforting to know.

Naomi was a little old-fashioned and of the Catholic faith. She was a kind, religious woman, an older lady with white hair, all done up in a bun on top of her head. She was quite a jolly soul, and she seemed to have a bright light around her; I could see the light shine in her eyes. She was kind to me, and we became great friends. She actually become like a mother figure to me, as I had no real family living close by. So when I returned home from the bank that day, I immediately called Naomi. She did not seem surprised by the events that were occurring in my life. I remember that she had warned me to be careful how I handled this situation. She knew my husband had an awful temper. She must have picked up on his negative energy. Honestly, who knew what he would do if he thought I was going to leave him and take the kids? And how was I going to accomplish that anyway?

The truth is, I am a strong personality myself, so of course I confronted my husband when he got home that evening. He confessed to me that he had made a deal with a guy at work that did not work out as planned. Who knows what it actually was this time? My husband had a difficult time when it came to our finances. He usually owed somebody money for something. He wasn't a horrible person, just irresponsible. This is not what I wanted for my family. I was fed up with his antics at this point; he had gone too far this time. I can say without a doubt that I was furious! I told him that was it! I was leaving and taking the children. (Sounds like a poorly scripted movie, right?)

Well, the whole idea of my leaving and taking the girls didn't go over well. The next thing I knew he had his hands around my throat and was choking me in the middle of the living room. This was one of those times in life when you just can't believe you have gotten yourself into such a mess. If it hadn't been for my four-year-old screaming at the top of her lungs for her father to stop, I probably would not be here writing this book today. When she started to scream, he just stopped, then she began to cry. I guess the yelling was loud and someone called the cops. The next thing I remember, the police were at the front door. My husband settled down and calmly opened the door. He spoke to the officers through the screen. We both calmed down, realizing we did not want any trouble. I told the police officers that I was OK. They gave us a verbal warning and left.

I had become good friends with my next-door neighbors, Pat and Sherry. Unfortunately, they were well aware of what a hot temper my husband had. Sherry would always say, "We don't need an alarm clock at our house; we wake up to his screaming every morning!" How embarrassing. I guess you just don't realize how bad the verbal abuse is until someone else says something about it. I suppose you get used to it. The verbal abuse had become part of our daily routine—a part of my children's everyday life.

The police's coming to our home had a huge impact on me. They must see this stuff all the time, but I did not grow up this way, and I definitely did not want my children to. I knew that I had to leave, but how was I going to go without his knowing? He might try to hurt me again. I thought long and hard on a plan of action. I made a decision to leave but without his realizing it. I let some time pass until things cooled down. In the meantime I swallowed my pride and called my parents in New Mexico. I told them that I was in a bad situation and that I needed to get out of it. They suggested that the kids and I come and stay with them. I had some vacation time coming at work, and my husband did not. I told him I was going to visit my parents with the girls. I did not tell him that I would make this a permanent vacation, but I had no plans of returning to Michigan.

During this time I prayed more than I had in a very long time. I asked for guidance and a better life for me and my children. No way were they going to grow up in this negative environment! I, like many people, did not want to give up all my worldly possessions. I started to slowly ship things to my parents' home—boxes of pictures, clothes, kids' toys, anything that meant something to me. One box at a time. Items that I knew my husband would not miss. I knew that when I left, I would have to give up the things that I left behind, but the stuff did not matter to me. I was ready to start a new, joyful life with my girls.

Naomi was my rock. She would say things to me like, "God only gives us what we can handle." She said that one day my white knight would come and I would have a great relationship. I held on to that dream and to my children.

There is another important thing that I want you to know about prayer: when you pray, always give thanks. Not just for what you have prayed for, but for what you already have. We should always acknowledge the blessings that we already have in our lives. I believe that God appreciates this just as you appreciate it when kind words of thanks are spoken to you.

Chapter 8

Faith Works!

I NEED TO ADDRESS faith if you are going to work with the Universal Energy. Faith and energy are things we cannot physically see. True unwavering faith is that God our Creator is taking care of our needs. True faith is a very difficult thing to achieve; it is being childlike and believing in what you cannot see.

Now faith is confidence in what we hope
for and assurance about what we do not see.
—Hebrews 11:1

Faith was a difficult concept for me to wrap my head around. How do you believe in something that you cannot touch or see? When life gives you lemons instead of lemonade, it is difficult to have confidence that everything will be taken care of for your highest good. This is when true unwavering faith is necessary. Before I continue to teach you more about the energy and how to use it, I feel I should tell you more of my story so that you understand how I learned to have faith and how I learned to use the energy to my benefit.

One afternoon I went to visit my friend Naomi. This is the day that I truly became aware of faith. She was such a kind soul to me when I needed someone to love and care about me. On this particular afternoon when I was visiting her, she said, "I have something for you." She had a gift for me. Naomi handed me a small box. Inside, wrapped in white tissue paper, was a little porcelain statue of a girl with blond braids that read "Faith Works." Naomi told me that this was to remind me to have faith in God, faith in God's plan for me. I put the small statue on my kitchen windowsill to remind me to have faith. This way, I saw her often and tried to remember what Naomi had said to me. I have to admit that I was not very faithful during this time. I was afraid and angry with the world. I was frustrated that I had gotten myself into such an unhealthy situation. I knew it was affecting me and my children's quality of life. I yearned to be happy.

Deciding to leave my second husband was probably my biggest leap of faith thus far, and I did not even realize it at the time. I had put faith in my decision to move out West with my girls to create a better life for us. I had also put faith in my parents that they would guide us as we moved to this new desert land, but I had not put my faith in the Lord. I have to be honest. I was not there yet, as I still felt I held the power over what happened in my life.

Here is a true story about another young family's faith that will make you a believer in the energy that faith holds. I have changed their names, as the couple wishes to remain anonymous. Joe and Lana were in their early thirties, with two young children and living in New Mexico. They had both grown up in Albuquerque and attended college at the University of New Mexico. Joe was in a dead-end job that he dreaded going to every day. Lana was a new mom and yearned to be able to stay home with their new baby girl and homeschool their older son. The reality was that all these things cost money and they were short on funds. They said that they wanted a new life where they could prosper with their children. They both felt stagnant in the same town where they had grown up and attended school. Joe wanted a better job with decent pay to take care of their little family.

Lana's grandparents suggested that they move to the Great Lakes state of Michigan. The grandparents assured them that the economy was better than in the Southwest. So they took a huge leap of faith and moved the entire family and their dog halfway across the country to the great Midwest.

Once they arrived, things were not as they had hoped. The job market in Joe's field of work was not what had been promised. He was forced to take a job outside his area of expertise. He had no choice—he had to feed the family. To Lana's disappointment, she, too, had to find a job because Joe's pay was not enough to take care of the bills. Lana's forty-five-minute drive in the cold Michigan winter took a toll on her and the kids. Joe's drive was no better. The house that they could afford was smaller than their home in Albuquerque had been, and the daycare costs were higher as well. Unfortunately, Lana's grandparents were not able to help out with the children as often as they had hoped. Lana said it had gotten to the point where she placed their last few dollars in the collection plate at church and asked God to help them financially. They put their faith in a Higher Power. Lana said that after her prayer, she had faith that the Lord would provide. As a result, some freelance marketing jobs were referred to Lana, one after another. The extra income helped immensely, but they still struggled. They both told me that even though they were struggling, they remained faithful, as the Lord had brought them this far. Lana told me that she prayed every day that God would show them the way.

They had lived in Michigan for over a year when the call came: Joe's mother had passed away suddenly. She had been ill, but nothing like this was ever expected. Joe was heartbroken. She had raised him as a single mom, and he had not had much interaction with his father. Joe and Lana loaded up the car to travel back to New Mexico to be with Joe's family and to handle his mother's affairs.

It's funny how God works. He seems to add light to tragedy and keep the faithful believing. As things turned out, in her will Joe's mother had left Joe her house, which was paid for. What a blessing for the young struggling family! Their friends and family expected them to sell the home and return to Michigan, but Joe and Lana both expressed to me that they felt the Lord had led them back to New Mexico for a reason. Things had not gone as smoothly as they had anticipated in Michigan.

When the energy does not flow as it is supposed to, you need to recognize the signs and change your path. That is exactly what Joe and Lana did. They took another leap of faith. They moved back to Albuquerque, where Joe found the job of his dreams and loves what he does to this day! Lana homeschools three days a week and enjoys being a housewife. They both told me that God had a plan for them and they are happy that they had the faith to recognize it. I am sure Joe's mom is looking down and smiling on them.

Our vacation date arrived. It seemed to take forever to come. I was excited and nervous all at the same time. I knew that this would be the last time I saw our house and the street we lived on. I also knew that this was the last time I would see my husband. It was strange and exciting all at once. I felt a sense of freedom when the plane finally lifted up off the runway in Detroit. I knew that we would not have to deal with this negative, abusive situation any longer.

Away we went on vacation to the Southwest, to New Mexico. I had never traveled out west before. Everything was different; I had not realized just how different it would be! The landscape was shades of brown and beige, and the people were different. The entire culture in New Mexico was a new experience. There were many Spanish people, cowboys, and real Native Americans. This was going to be a whole new way of life for us.

I had not seen my parents in quite some time, so to visit with them was nice. They looked well and were happy to see us. We spent the first few days catching up and getting to know each other again. It had been quite a few years since I had spent any quality time with my parents. I had decided not to tell my husband that this was a permanent vacation right away. I needed a little peace in my life before all hell broke loose.

When I did finally did tell him, I felt terrible. He was heartbroken. I felt so bad for him that I decided to return to Michigan to give the relationship one last try. Sometimes I wonder why God gave me such a big heart. It has gotten me in trouble more times than I can tell you. It's difficult to act with your head and not with your heart. This thing called life was not so easy for me. Naomi told me that this was a mistake, but I did not listen to her. I don't think my parents knew what to say. I think they just wanted us to be happy and secure.

My husband flew to New Mexico, and we all drove back together. I figured I had to give our marriage one last try. As time passed, things went back to the way they had been; nothing had changed.

I have come to realize that many people go through this same scenario. They leave their spouses and then return because they remember only the good times. Most are hoping things will be different because the person they think they love says they will be different. This is nothing to be ashamed of. I think most of us do not want a relationship or a marriage to fail and will do what it takes to stay together, even when it's not healthy.

Well, our relationship did not improve. We were text-book. My situation just became worse, and I ended up leaving him anyway.

I have some advice for everyone reading this: people rarely change. They are who they are. You have a choice to accept them as they are or not. Know that you cannot change another person. The person has to want to change themself, and not for you but for themself. Huge lesson for me!

My friend Sherry and her husband, Pat, who had lived next door to us previously, took all three of us in when my husband became violent again. They had since moved to Auburn Hills and had built a new home. They knew what I was dealing with and were wonderful to me and the kids. We stayed with them for a few months until I got back on my feet financially. I hope they know how much I appreciated their help. Sherry and I have remained good friends over the years; Pat has since passed. God bless them both for helping me and the girls. I am forever grateful.

I found a great job and was able to rent an apartment for the kids and me. With my parents' help, I filed for divorce and moved on with my life. I was making good money, but with the cost of daycare for two children, our rent, and the utilities, I barely had enough money left for food. I didn't receive any type of consistent child support in those days. Money was tight, and it was a struggle for us to make it. To help out, my parents and Crystal's grandparents (from my first marriage) bought things that the girls needed along the way. Everyone always seemed to pitch in just as I needed them to in those days. I learned to appreciate the small things. I phoned Naomi every Sunday and spoke with her about the week's events. She knew from our conversations that I was having a tough time making it. She would say to me, "Come over and see me and I will give you some groceries to help you out." The kids loved to go to her house, and I did too. We had become great friends, and I loved to talk with her. She always had treats for the girls, candy and such. She and I would go down into her basement, and she would ask what I needed—flour or cereal for the kids? She would fill grocery bags full of food for me to take home. She had a freezer down there, too, with all kinds of meats and frozen goods. I will never forget those days that Naomi helped me when I was so tight on funds. I do not know what I would have done without her. She taught me how important it is to give to others in need.

At Christmastime she would put together treat bags full of candy for the girls. She bought small trinkets and wrapped them up for them so that it seemed as if they had more presents to open on Christmas morning. One of my fondest memories of Naomi is her Christmas tradition of dipping pretzels in white chocolate. She made the best pretzels covered in white chocolate that I have ever had in my life! I can almost taste the white chocolate as I write this. She always had a bag for me to take home. I love them to this day. You remember the small things when people are gone. Naomi is gone now, but when I have one of those pretzels, I think of how kind she was to us. I know she did not have much herself, but she always made sure we did not go without. I miss her light and her kind smile. I know she still watches over me.

Naomi knew that I was not the type to get on any kind of public assistance. I guess I never even considered it, as I have always felt I could make my own way. I made decent money and probably too much to receive any kind of assistance anyway. I did not receive much child support. Yes, I was supposed to receive child support according to my divorce decree, but my older daughter's father did not make very much money. He was out of state and going to school. He had thirty-five dollars taken out of his paycheck weekly, so I would receive a check for seventy dollars every two weeks. I know it does not sound like much, but those child support checks every couple of weeks really helped us. My recent ex-husband did not send money very often. I did, however, receive his tax refund a couple of times. His refund always seemed to show up through the years just when I needed it the most. The Universe always timed it just right for me.

I was working for one of the automakers when I realized I had to make a change. I really loved my job. I was the sales coordinator for a sales team, selling our component parts to other car manufacturers. The only problem with this scenario was that I would drop the girls off at latchkey (the early-school program) in the dark at six o'clock in the morning, then pick them up in the dark Michigan winter at six o'clock at night. This was not only hard on me, but it was hard on my daughters. I did this for many months until I finally decided I had to make a change.

Chapter 9

Just Ask! And Be Grateful!

IT MAY SEEM SILLY to remind you to ask for what you want, but you would be surprised at how many of us simply don't ask. I don't recall how I started to ask—probably through prayer. I would ask God for the big things when something was going haywire in my life. Then I learned as time passed that it was OK to request the smaller things as well. Before I go into a tough meeting, I will say, "God please let this meeting go smoothly and benefit all involved." And the meeting will go incredibly well. I have learned to be specific in my requests. I have experimented with asking. I learned that the Universe gives you exactly what you order, so be careful what you say. Now, if what you're asking for is not for your highest good, you will not get your wish. You will get what you need, which may be something even better than you requested, and the outcome may surprise you. The power is in the energy of the spoken word. You give the words energy when you speak them. The vibration and the intention of your words goes out into the Universe. The same vibration is eventually returned back to you.

When I have an issue to resolve and need to make a phone call go my way, I always say a prayer before I make the call. Sometimes I will pray to my angels. They are all around you and will assist you immediately. The Universe has rules to this game: the intention has to be good for all involved, and it has to be an honorable request. You can say something like, "Make sure I get the perfect person on the line—someone who will help me reach my goal." This works every time!

I remember my older sister Judy telling me that she did not ask God for anything, because she felt that she had enough. This was very honorable of her, but what the Universe has shown me is that God wants you to ask for what you desire. The goal is for us to be happy, joyful, and fulfilled. I told her it was OK to ask, that we were supposed to ask, but I don't think she ever did. She is with God now, happy and at peace.

Go ahead, take that leap of faith, and ask for the new house, the new car if you need one, and the perfect mate if that's what you desire. If things in your life are not as you want them to be, only you have the power to change them. The Universe is your canvas: create the picture that you want for yourself. However you paint your life is how it will be. Paint it, and watch it materialize.

Imagine that you are in a play and you are the director. You have the power to write your own script, the scene and the dialogue, to what you want your life to be. Many people have asked me if it's all right to make a request for someone else's benefit. (I look at it as a prayer.) Of course it is, but if it's not for their highest good, it won't happen. The Lord always knows what's best for us, even when we do not. There may be a lesson to be learned and you don't realize it. Remember, we are on this planet to develop our souls.

I have witnessed numerous people reinventing themselves successfully. They accomplished this by changing how they think, simply asking for what they want, and believing with unwavering faith that they would receive it or something even better. They learned how to reprogram their minds to think and receive positive thoughts and reject the negative ones. Ask God for what you desire, and expect to receive what you have asked for or something better. Ask, believe, and give thanks.

The Universe Rewards Us for Our Gratitude

The energy of giving and receiving is recognized by the Universe. The Universe also recognizes the energy when you are grateful for what you have received. The vibration of your energy lets the Universe know if you are truly grateful.

Have you ever heard the saying "You get what you give"? This short saying is true. When you do nice things for others for unselfish reasons, the Universe will reward you tenfold. On the opposite side of the spectrum, I have witnessed selfish people who are takers pay for not knowing how the Universe works. God our Creator rewards or punishes good and evil respectively. You can call it karmic energy, if you will. There are many lessons to learn in this lifetime. Learning to be grateful is one of them. Being appreciative for your good health and well-being creates good karmic energy.

"Therefore I tell you, whatever you ask for in prayer, believe that you have received it, and it will be yours. And when you stand praying, if you hold anything against anyone, forgive them, so that your Father in heaven may forgive you your sins."
—Mark 11:24–25

I grew up in an upper-middle-class American household. My father was a worker, by which I mean he was driven. My father is one of the most hard-working, honest, giving men that I know, other than my husband. He wanted to provide the best for his family. I am blessed to have a father like this. He worked a full-time job as an engineer during the day and farmed one hundred acres of soybeans at night and on the weekends. I did not see my father as much as I would have liked to when I was growing up. While he was working, my sisters and I enjoyed the latest fashions and the greatest toys and gadgets of the day. We weren't spoiled, but we never went without anything. I am grateful that I have such a wonderful father. As I reflect back on my youth, I wonder how different I would be if I had gotten to spend more quality time with my father. He's a great guy, and I would have truly enjoyed spending more time with him. I think there is a fine line between providing for your family and spoiling your family with too many material items. If truth be told, I would rather have spent more time with my father than had all the extra stuff. My older sister Judy used to say, "You come into this world with nothing, and you leave with nothing." I was often a bit puzzled by her remark until I realized that the people in your life are what truly matter in the end.

It wasn't until I was married, with my own children, that I realized how much it costs to live comfortably. This realization was a rude awakening for me, growing up as I did in my upper-middle-class family. I believe that you learn to appreciate things and are thankful for what you have only when you go without. You learn to be grateful when you have to struggle to purchase what you want and need on your own. The Universe is able to pick up on the energy when you are thankful for what you have. Our Creator set it up as a self-activating reward system for doing the right thing. Isn't that perfect?

Folks in our society have become takers rather than givers. Why has this happened? Have we become a selfish society? I need to let everyone know that there is a certain feeling that comes over you when you give unselfishly. It's a feeling of joy that you experience only when you have done a good deed for another human being. There are pleasure endorphins that are released into your body when you give freely to others. What I have discovered is that the more we give, the happier we become. What a concept! The energy is flowing as it was intended. It's amazing what God can do. Giving creates more giving. Now everyone who reads this knows how to change their lives for the better! Just give more to others, and be grateful for what you have. Giving thanks was spoken about often in the Bible. Sometimes we forget to be thankful. We are reminded of this in Psalms:

Give thanks to the Lord, for he is good.
His love endures forever.

—Psalm 136:1

Eldon Taylor, the author of *Choices and Illusions*, says that "a good way to learn the power of thankfulness and the satisfaction in helping others is to do one good deed a day for someone."[24] He suggests that you write down your daily good deed in a journal and reflect on it before bedtime. I believe that this exercise changes the energy in your body. The positive reinforcement endorphins are released into your body. These endorphins are pleasurable and good for your health.

Our Creator developed this so that we would feel good about giving and continue to do so more often. Learning to give back and learning to be grateful take work. Think of the famous Christmas story of Ebenezer Scrooge and what he had to go through to learn to give. We have all encountered someone who has a little Scrooge in them. They simply have not learned the lesson yet.

A great way to remember to be thankful is to place a chalkboard in your home or office. Put it in a space that you see often. At the top of the board write, "I am thankful for _____," then write down whatever you are thankful for that day; write something new each day. This exercise will remind you of how blessed you are. You can do a similar exercise by writing in a journal daily. Keep the journal by your bedside to reflect on the many blessings in your life as they happen. These few verses from Corinthians really sum it up:

Remember this: Whoever sows sparingly will also reap sparingly, and whoever sows generously will also reap generously. Each of you should give what you have decided in your heart to give, not reluctantly or under compulsion, for God loves a cheerful giver. And God is able to bless you abundantly, so that in all things at all times, having all that you need, you will abound in every good work. As it is written:

"They have freely scattered their gifts to the poor; their righteousness endures forever."

—2 Corinthians 9:6–9

Please understand how this law of giving and receiving works. The law of the Universe is that you will reap what you sow. When you give something to a person or an organization, do it anonymously if possible, and with no conditions. The lesson here is to always give freely. No strings attached. Do not expect anything in return for your generosity. Do not expect that the money you give to a friend or family member will be returned. If you expect the money back, you are setting yourself up for disappointment. People often don't or can't repay their debts. If you are going to loan someone money, do not plan on receiving it back. Give it freely; there will be no hard feelings when you follow this rule. Money can create good and bad energy, depending upon the intention.

Chapter 10

Use Your Energy to Forgive If You Want to Be Forgiven

I FEEL THAT I need to address forgiveness and the energy that accompanies the act. As I have discovered, many people have a difficult time forgiving each other. Forgiveness has been a lesson for me that was hard to achieve. Someone would do me wrong, and I would just hold on to it. I could not and would not let go of that angry energy. I held the old grudge energy. I would say, "Well that's it! I will not have anything to do with that person." I would cut them out of my life completely. As a result, I would end up holding on to the negativity that was created by the situation—the negative energy. This type of behavior is not healthy for you mentally or physically. I have come to realize that holding a grudge solves nothing. Holding on keeps the negative energy swirling all around inside you.

The person who taught me this important lesson in life is the man whom I am happily married to today. I had never met anyone before this man who showed me, by example, that forgiveness is essential for you to move forward in life. He taught me that forgiveness has nothing to do with the other person who has caused you pain; the forgiveness is for you. He also reminded me of this passage in the Bible that addresses this very subject:

"For if you forgive other people when they sin against you, your heavenly Father will also forgive you. But if you do not forgive others their sins, your Father will not forgive your sins."

—Matthew 6:14

I now understood that I had to swallow my pride and learn to forgive others. Let me remind you that none of us is perfect. We all make mistakes along life's journey. This is how all of us learn. It is not an easy lesson to learn, but it is extremely important to understand that you have to forgive people if you want to be forgiven. If you don't forgive and let go of the negativity, the bad energy remains with you. That's why it is so important to forgive. You are helping yourself by releasing the bad vibes that resonate within your energy field.

What the Universe has revealed to me regarding forgiveness is that when a person intentionally does something mean or evil to you, the karmic energy of that act goes back to them tenfold. In other words, they get what's coming to them. You don't have to do anything at all. God takes care of this for you. You may not see this happen for a long time or maybe not even in your lifetime. But it does happen, I can assure you. I recognized that this is how the Universal Energy flows. I have witnessed this in my life and in my friends' and family's lives. I realized that I don't have to do anything to retaliate when someone is hateful and ugly towards me. The Universal Energy takes care of this for you. When you hold on to the negativity that the act created, you are hurting yourself. The other person has accomplished their goal. They are winning!

I do understand how hard it is to forgive someone. It takes a lot of inner strength to do so. It takes more inner strength to forgive someone than it does not to. The loved ones and family members of a person killed by another person are heartbroken by the loss. They have a difficult time forgiving. I understand their anguish and their desire for justice and/or revenge, but I pray for them to realize that the killer will get what's coming to him or her. The killer's punishment may be many years in jail, or it may be having to live with the guilt of what they have done. The mental anguish associated with any wrongdoing can often be worse than death. The anguished loved ones and family need to be assured that this will be taken care of on their behalf. It's how the energy flows; the Universe is consistent.

Here is a wonderful story which demonstrates the power and the energy of forgiveness: It was 1997, and Greg and Cathy were living in Huna, Alaska. Greg's knee had been bothering him. He'd had previous issues with his knee and was hoping the pain would ease and disappear. When it did not, he made an appointment with a local doctor. The doctor confirmed that he had a ripped ACL (anterior cruciate ligament) The ACL is one of the four main ligaments within the knee that connects the femur to the tibia. He also had issues with his meniscus. Greg needed surgery to correct the problems immediately. Since Greg and Cathy lived on an island in a remote area of Alaska, they made the decision to travel back to their hometown of Albuquerque for the surgery. Greg was very fond of his orthopedic surgeon, who had treated him previously back at Presbyterian Hospital in New Mexico; Greg said he felt comfortable with this doctor. It was close to the Thanksgiving holiday when Greg flew into the Albuquerque airport. Cathy had stayed behind since their children were still in school.

Greg's mom drove him to meet with the doctor. The surgeon confirmed that he would need an operation to repair the ACL by screwing it to the bone. They would check his meniscus at the same time. Surgery was set for 6:00 a.m. The orthopedic surgeon explained that the surgery was routine and that Greg could have therapy to rehabilitate his knee when he returned home to Alaska. The day arrived, and the surgery was a success! Greg was able to go home the next day. Cathy had flown in for the operation, and she drove him to his mother's house in the Albuquerque area to recuperate. He was instructed to return for a follow-up visit with his doctor in three days.

Greg had been home a day or so when his knee became severely inflamed. He was in a tremendous amount of pain. He could not move his leg. They contacted the doctor and were told to meet the surgeon at the emergency room immediately. Upon Greg's arrival, the doctor was there to greet them and examined his knee. To the surgeon's surprise, Greg had a staph infection. They admitted him to the hospital and immediately drained the infection. In order to treat the infection properly, they sent a sample to the lab for analysis to determine what type of staph infection Greg had. They brought in a specialist, a disease doctor, to help. The specialist was not able to determine what type of infection it was.

In the meantime, Greg was prepped for surgery. He had to be sedated for them to drain his knee and flush out the infection. Greg went through this same process every other day for a week; he would rest for a day and then return to surgery to repeat the procedure. When Friday arrived, the surgeon told Greg that they were unable to treat the staph infection. The doctor told Greg that his leg would have to be amputated on Monday morning. Greg told me he was devastated. He is an electrician by trade. He wondered how he was going to continue with his career and his lifestyle in Alaska with his leg partially removed.

It was Sunday night when his father came to visit him in the hospital. His father was a very religious man. He stayed with Greg to comfort him and to pray with him in his time of need. Not too long after his father left the hospital, his old friend and a minister, George, came to pray with him also. Before George left that night, he told Greg that the Lord had told him that Greg would have a "visitor" that night and not to be afraid. Greg naturally shrugged it off, as he was about to have his leg amputated the next morning.

This is what Greg told me happened to him. He said it was maybe midnight or one o'clock in the morning when a brilliant bright light entered his hospital room. He said he could no longer hear the sounds of the machines that he was connected to. He said everything just stopped, and he heard an audible voice say, "Do not be afraid. Everything is going to be fine. Your knee will be healed as long as you follow my instructions."

Greg said he was not afraid and felt a sense of peace in his soul. He explained to me that he did not see a figure, only the bright light that had entered his room. The voice said, "These are the things that you are doing wrong in your life." Greg was instructed to forgive his brother and another man for any ill will that he held against them and to apologize to these two men. He was told to join a church and to attend worship services every Sunday. He was instructed to tithe regularly and be baptized again. The voice said that he was to come back to the hospital on Thursday at 1:00 p.m.

After these instructions were given to him, Greg said the light was gone and he could hear the monitors in the room start beeping again. He was in shock and amazement by what had just happened to him. He told me that when the morning came and the nurse arrived to wheel him down for surgery, she said in a surprised tone, "How did you get so tan? It looks like your face is sunburned." Greg knew why he was tanned: it was the powerful bright light that had visited him last night, but he did not say a word.

When Greg awakened from his surgery, the doctor told him that he did not know what had happened but that the infection was completely gone from his leg and his leg did not need to be amputated. The nurses were in disbelief as well, but Greg knew what had happened. He had been given a second chance, a chance to forgive two important people in his life and a chance to live a different life than he had lived before. The only thing that puzzled him was why he was supposed to go back to the hospital on Thursday at 1:00 p.m.

Greg was released the next day to go home. His family was relieved and full of joy, as he still had his leg and was healed. He explained to me that he told his wife what had happened to him. He was adamant that she drive him back to the hospital on Thursday at 1:00 p.m. She did as he asked. They arrived at the hospital and took the elevator up to the floor where he had been a patient. He said that he stepped off the elevator, crutches in hand, a few minutes before one o'clock. He immediately saw the nurses and the staff that had taken care of him. To his amazement, they were all there. They surrounded him and hugged him. He told me there were many tears of joy for him from the staff. He said that as he looked around, he saw that everybody who had taken care of him through his ordeal was there. He couldn't believe it! He asked, "Why are you all here at the same time?" They laughed and replied, "It's shift change for us, that's why we are all here and able to see you." He explained to me that he felt that the Lord wanted the staff at the hospital to know of the miracle that had occurred.

Greg told me that he has forgiven his brother and the other man and that he was baptized again. He attends church every Sunday, and he tithes on a regular basis. Greg said that when he forgave, it was as if a burden had been lifted from his soul. He also mentioned that he is not fearful, as he knows that the Lord is near, and that he lives life today to its fullest.

The Dalai Lama says:

> It would be much more constructive if people tried
> to understand their supposed enemies. Learning to
> forgive is much more useful than merely picking up
> a stone and throwing it at the object of one's anger,
> the more so when the provocation is extreme. For
> it is under the greatest adversity that there exists
> the greatest potential for doing good, both for
> oneself and others. When we are able to recognize
> and forgive ignorant actions done in one's past, we
> strengthen ourselves and can solve the problems of
> the present constructively.[25]

I look forward to the day when people have attained a
higher consciousness and realize that when they do others
wrong, the negative energy will be returned to them tenfold.
When folks actually get this lesson, they won't dare attack
another human being again. People just have not figured this
little fact out yet. As the human race evolves, they will realize
it, and then the violence on our planet will stop.

Chapter 11

Material Possessions Do
Not Bring Happiness

WHEN I MOVED TO New Mexico, I began to realize that material possessions were not so important. I had lost many things along the way. This is when I realized that things could be replaced. This was actually a blessing, as it was good to buy new things. The old things held the old memories as well as the bad energy attached to them. The change was good for me and the girls, a fresh start for us. We loved our new furniture, and we had so much fun decorating in southwestern décor. What the Universe revealed to me is that things can be replaced. But you, your children, your loved ones, and your sanity cannot be. I wanted my daughters to grow up in a healthy, loving environment. I think that's what most people want for their children.

This subject has really hit home with me. We all attend school to receive an education, and then we work hard to have a nice place to live, a reliable car, and all the things that we are taught should make us happy—the American Dream. I have spoken with so many people who say that when they get that this or thing that they have worked so hard for, they will be happy. But when they reach their goal, there's always something new that they desire that will make them happier yet. There is something still lacking inside their soul. They still want more things. Things do not fulfill your soul! Stuff does not last forever, but your soul's energy does.

We have all been at a point in our lives when we really wanted something. Maybe it was a new outfit, a car, or a new house. Now think back . . . back to when you finally got that thing you really wanted more than anything in the world. When you received it and the excitement and the newness wore off, did that thing lose its exciting energy? Most often this is what happens. The thing just does not seem to be so great after all. The newness has worn off.

I have witnessed this behavior and experienced this attempt at fulfillment with material items myself. I see this scenario with a large percentage of our country's young people. They want the new phone, the newest style in clothes, the money, the house, and the new car. And what's wrong with that? The problem is that the media's and the Internet's influence on our youth in America has been to teach them that the one who dies with the most stuff wins!

I realized that what mattered most to me were the people in my life: my children, family, and friends. Stuff can be replaced, but the people in your life cannot be.

For the love of money is a root of all kinds of evil.
Some people, eager for money, have wandered from
the faith and pierced themselves with many griefs.

—1 Timothy 6:10

Even after the economic downturn in our country, I still see many people on the material path. I believe that many folks did get the message, and if you are one of them, count your blessings. Some people will just never figure it out.

There is an old saying, "You can't take it with you." This is so true. Why not share the wealth with other people who are really needy and suffering while here on planet earth? There are numerous families in America and abroad that cannot feed their children or buy proper clothing for them to wear. They are not able to pay their basic utility bills. Why not share your wealth with the less fortunate? The energy that you will receive back from unselfishly helping others comes back to you tenfold. What a good feeling it is to give to another human being! To know that you have truly helped another person is true fulfillment of the soul.

Simply put, the Universe has revealed to me that the love you have in your heart for others and the kindness you give to people daily are the real riches in this life. If you can accomplish this, you will be one of the richest humans on this planet.

The Universe has made me Wake Up! and realize that once you get the car, the house, the money, and all the stuff, if you don't have loved ones to share it with, then it doesn't matter how much you have accumulated in your lifetime. Now when I say "loved ones," I mean people in your life who care about you whether you are wealthy or a pauper. True friendship does not have a price tag on it. The same goes for family members. Just because someone is a member of your family does not mean that they are looking out for your best interest or sending you good energy. Usually people are looking out for their own best interest. But sometimes you find people who are willing to help you unconditionally. My parents are two of those people who helped me when I needed it the most.

My parents suggested that I move to New Mexico again, permanently this time. I was grateful for their help. They would take the girls to school and pick them up so that I could go to work. I agreed. I needed a car and wanted to bring some of our things with me. I had given up most of my belongings when I left the first time, so I did not want to leave everything behind this time. After our divorce, my ex-husband had gotten rid of many of our things, which I had expected to happen, but you still feel violated. After several discussions with my parents, we decided that my father would fly to Michigan and drive out west with the kids and me.

And so our journey back to the Wild West began. My father took Crystal with him in a rented a U-Haul truck, and Samantha rode with me in the car. The trip went smoothly. We traveled three or four days, crossing several states before we reached the "Land of Enchantment"—that's what they call New Mexico. As I think back on it, most of the events of the trip are a blur to me. I believe that happens sometimes in life when things are not good. You seem to just go with it. What happens is that your mind hides the bad somewhere in your subconscious. I believe it's a protection mechanism so that you can press on in life and move forward without losing your wits.

Reflecting back on that time, I realized that God did not want me to live in Michigan any longer; he wanted me to live in New Mexico. He had tried to move me there earlier, but I thought I knew better than He did. My mistake.

When things are not going smoothly in business or in a relationship, something has to change. It simply means you're just not on the right path. It has taken me years to figure this out. In other words, if you are on the right path, life will go smoothly for you. Things will just fall into place easily: You meet the right people. You are in the right places at the right time. The energy flows. But when you are not on your path, the road gets extremely bumpy, and you have to change course whether you want to or not. The Universe just seems to make it happen that way. You are here on earth for a short lifetime. Use your intuition, and always do what feels right while you are here; if your path feels uncomfortable, change course.

I have confirmation that all things really do happen for a reason. I know people say it all the time, but I have lived it. I may not have been able to understand the events that were taking place at the time. Reflecting back, however, I realize that I was exactly where I was supposed to be at that point in my life. This was not an accident; God had planned this for me.

I have realized that God presents us with lessons to learn and that if we don't get a lesson the first time, the Universal Energy will present the same lesson to us again. It's a do-over.

I was doing this lesson over because I just did not get it the first time. I was relocating to New Mexico again because that is where I was supposed to be months ago.

The Lord has blessed us humans with free will. He tries hard to make us see the light the first time so that we don't have to repeat the lesson. We do, however, make our own choices. Life lessons are always difficult to learn, but I now realize that growth occurs with every lesson learned.

Please do not confuse *the Universe* with *God*. God created the Universe. He created the Universal Energy to work with us and to keep us in check. My daughter Crystal often corrects me when I say the Universe did this or that. She will say, "You mean God." And I will reply yes. I mean God who created the Universe. Our Creator controls the Universe and its energy flow to all living things.

My girls seemed to settle in well at my parents' house, which was a big relief. My goal was to find a job and get my own place. If you have ever had to move back home with your parents after being married and having children, it is a very difficult thing to do—humbling, to say the least! You feel as if you are going backwards in life. I had to swallow my independent pride and bite my tongue numerous times. Although I was appreciative, I had not lived at home for a very long time. Things were different, and my parents were different. They had a certain way of doing things, which I found out very quickly. There were things I did not know about my parents.

My father was more particular than I had ever realized. Maybe I wasn't paying attention too closely while I was growing up. Had he always been like this? We adapted to his methodical ways while living in their home. My father had recently retired from an engineering career after thirty-five years. He was still consulting from home, so our arrival added to his retirement duties.

Mom seemed different too. She had begun collecting these little wind-up toys that she kept in a box under her bed. She would pull the toys out to entertain the kids from time to time. When did she start collecting these? Who was this person who had always seemed so prim and proper and was now pulling out the most awesome toys to make the girls smile?

My mother would also offer her opinion about raising my children. Sometimes I agreed, sometimes not so much. Don't get me wrong: my parents were wonderful people to help me and my children through a tough transition. I mean, I realize that this whole thing was a sacrifice for them as well. But I would raise my daughters my way. I think most parents feel that way.

It is difficult moving back home to your parents' house. I know that's the second time I have said that, but let's just be honest: you do seem to feel a sense of failure going back home, even though you know deep down inside that you are not. It really wasn't that terrible; I had to swallow my pride more than I wanted to. Now I look back and thank God I had a place to go and parents who cared about me enough to take us in. The situation was difficult for us, but the girls and I made the best of it, and my parents did too.

Since my dad had recently retired, I knew our moving in was a disruption in his life plan. But I think he enjoyed having the kids around and helping them with their home-work and school projects. My dad was famous when it came to creating science-fair-project winners. He was always there to help the girls when I could not be. He was a much-needed positive male figure in their lives, and I am grateful for his influence on them.

My mother was always there for them as well. She had snacks ready for them when they got home from school and made sure they did their homework and cleaned up their rooms. My mom took care of the laundry and had their school clothes ready for the next day. She cooked many din-ners for us, as I would get home late many evenings. I hope they know how grateful I was for their help. Although we were happy staying at my parents' home, I did not want to live with them for too long. As I mentioned before, I am an independent soul and wanted to raise my daughters to be independent little ladies.

After a few weeks, I was fortunate to get a job at a gyp-sum company. The employment agency that I had signed up with found a position for me rather quickly. I was so relieved to have a well-paying job with benefits. My new company paid the employment agency its finder's fee, and I became a permanent hire. I was grateful to them for the opportunity.

The man who hired me was very knowledgeable about the gypsum business. He and I had a good rapport. My imme-diate supervisor was a whole different story. This woman was really quite difficult to get along with from the start. She was about my age or slightly younger. She had received her sales and management training from the military. I feel as if, for whatever reason, she just did not like me from the beginning. She did her best on a daily basis to make me feel uncomfortable and not part of the group. She would make remarks to try to cut me down in the office and let me know that she was my boss and that I was definitely beneath her. The whole atmosphere was weird. I guess you could say there was an abundance of negative energy swirling around the place.

Here's some employment background on me: I had worked for large corporations in management positions at this point in my professional career. I had been a buyer for a department store chain, traveling in and out of New York City; I had worked for one of the Big Three automakers in Michigan; I had been a consultant for Revlon in West Germany; and I had managed numerous retail stores. I am a conscientious lady, I am extremely independent, and I rarely take any guff. I have good manners, great morals, and upstanding values. I definitely knew how to play the political work game. I guess I can be intimidating at times, but that has never been my intention. I have learned over time to stand up for myself. I had to learn this lesson early in life, or I would have been trampled upon a long time ago.

The energy at the gypsum company continued to feel bad. Things were just not going smoothly at the office. I started to hate going to work. My boss's attitude grew worse as I learned to do my job more proficiently. This woman just did not like me and was making my life miserable. I am still not sure to this day what possessed her to be so mean to me. The lesson here for me was to never treat anyone else in this manner. Treat people as you would want to be treated, and the good energy will flow.

I started to question God again. Why was I here working at this place? What was I meant to be doing? Why was this happening to me? I was not very happy at this job, but I had to stick it out. I needed the money. I still had my little statue, "Faith Works," that Naomi had given me. Now she sat on the dresser at my parents' home. I kept hoping, but I really had not bought into the whole idea yet.

I made up my mind: I was not going to be miserable every day. I refused to let the mean girl at the office succeed. I picked up the newspaper and started to look for a new position. I saw an ad in the newspaper for a manager of a new denim store opening in town. I had tons of retail management experience, and the store was a block away from my parents' house! I would apply. Thanks to God, they called me right away. I interviewed for the manager position and got the job! The new store paid more money than the gypsum company did, and I was closer to home. And this time I was the boss. I was so grateful to be able to move forward. It was a happy day for me when I gave my notice at the gypsum company. I did feel bad, however, that they had paid such a large fee for me to work for them. Maybe they would recognize why I had moved on and they would make some changes in personnel for the next person who held my position. What I came to realize is that each time I stood up for myself, I moved forward in life. The energy was getting better.

Chapter 12

The Universe Presents Us
with Lessons to Learn

HAVE YOU EVER NOTICED that if you don't get the lesson the first time, the Universe will put the same scenario in front of you until you get it right? Think about it. Have you had to relive the same relationship more than once or had the same thing happen to you at a job repeatedly? This has happened to me many times. As you realize this is occurring, you start to understand that maybe somebody is trying to tell you something. What I have come to realize is that we all have lessons to learn while on this planet, and until we get the lesson, it will be presented to us repeatedly until we get it right. The Universe recognizes the energy flow determined by whether you got the lesson this time. If not, it will be presented to you again. The same lesson will be presented with a different person or a different job, for example, but it will be the same scenario. It's up to you to change the outcome, to learn from your experience.

A very wise friend clued me in to this fact several years ago. She recognized the pattern in me. I was feeling as if I were reliving the same scenario multiple times but with different people. She said to me, "Don't you see that the same thing keeps happening to you because you have not changed your behavior, your reactions, your belief?" God will continue to put the same situation in front of us until we grasp what He is teaching us. This has occurred not only in my personal life but in my business practice as well. The Universe has a way of teaching us life lessons without our realizing it.

There are many scenarios in life where this occurs. For example, you meet someone and you think they are the one, the perfect mate. Then, when things don't work out as planned, you are surprised. What happened? If you are attracting the same type of relationship into your life that does not work out, then you have a lesson to learn about yourself. Once you learn the relationship lesson, then you will move on to a healthier one. The Universe picks up on your energy. It can gauge the energy to determine whether you got the lesson presented to you or not. Relationships, whether in love or in business, are not always easy. You could be attracting what you think is good for you, but in reality it's not the best thing for your life. The Universal Energy was created for our benefit. All we have to do is pay attention.

If you are attracting the same situation or relationship into your life repeatedly, there must be a lesson for you to learn. Once you realize the lesson and change your behavior, the situation will change for the better. Everything works out as it should. Lessons are difficult to swallow, but growth occurs with every lesson. It is important for you to pay attention. Even though it may be difficult to do, recognize what is happening in your life. There may be a lesson for you.

Remember that God wants only the best for His children. The Universe is telling you that a situation didn't work out because it wasn't for your highest good. There is something or someone out there who is better for you. Here is what happened to me and how I figured this out.

I was opening up the new denim store in Albuquerque, and it was exciting! My retail background had allowed me this opportunity. I interviewed and hired an awesome staff of salespeople. The designer clothing line we carried was top-notch. The employees of the company received a hefty discount on all the designer labels. This was a wonderful incentive for the crew. The store was close to home and the kids' school. I started to feel good about life again. I worked hard, and the people I worked for were great! It was a family-owned business, and they seemed to genuinely care about their employees. After six months or so they told me that we were moving our independent store to the mall. I was excited! If things went well, I would make more money for my little family.

In the mist of all the excitement of my new job came the call. Crystal's father, my first husband, Claude, had gone into cardiac arrest back in Michigan. We received the news in the fall, and I was in total disbelief. Claude and I were the same age. We had been high-school sweethearts. I wasn't quite sure how he could have had a heart attack. Was this even possible? He was such a young man. What had happened to him? There were many unanswered questions. I made reservations for Crystal and me to fly to Michigan as soon as possible.

Crystal and I made the all-day trip to Michigan. My work was very supportive and gave me some time off. We arrived at the hospital to find Claude in a comatose state. He was in bed with his eyes open, looking right at me when we walked in the hospital room. The only problem was that he could not see me or hear me. Have you ever heard the saying, "The lights are on, but nobody's home"? Well, such was the case for Claude. This was a very difficult situation in my life to deal with.

Claude and I had gotten married young, and I always felt terrible that our marriage had failed. It was not due to a lack of love for each other; it was due to Claude's addiction to alcohol. He loved alcohol more than he loved himself or me. People have different vices in life, and alcohol had become his. I was aware of his addiction after we were married, but I never expected anything like this to happen to him.

The doctors would not tell me anything, as Claude and I were no longer husband and wife and Crystal was only ten years old at the time. We finally understood, after many questions, that the cause of Claude's coma had been a heart attack caused by his taking a combination of drugs and alcohol. They had tried to revive him several times and probably should not have accomplished their goal with the final resuscitation. As a result of the numerous resuscitations, he was left in a comatose state. It was devastating to watch someone

I loved so dearly be in a coma. He was an awesome person, always full of life and laughter and very creative. This whole situation just did not seem real. He looked just fine, better than he had in years, but he just could not utter a word, and he could not respond to anything around him. This was a very strange thing to be a part of and a very helpless place to be in. Crystal and I stayed with him for as long as we could. I hope he knew we were there with him. I believe he did. Before we left for home, I whispered in his ear that I loved him and that it was OK for him to go and be with God. I told him that I would always take care of our daughter, and I have always kept that promise to him.

This was a very sad time for us, and it is very hard for me to write about now. As I look back on the events of that time, I thank God that I had the ability to take Crystal to see her father. Claude lay in a comatose state for ten years and then went to be with the Lord.

When Crystal and I arrived back in New Mexico, I made a decision for our little family: it was time for us to move. This move was overdue; the girls and I were still living at my parents' house, and it was time for us to have a place of our own. I think every family needs their own space. After some searching, I found a very nice apartment for the girls and me. The next thing you know, I was learning about consignment stores. My mom clued me in to the concept. At consignment stores I could buy nice secondhand furniture that looked brand new at lower prices. The furniture was reasonably priced so that I could afford some nice stuff to furnish our new home. The people who consign make a profit, and so does the store. Well, this worked out beautifully. We were moving forward. I felt we were finally on the right path. The reason I am mentioning this is that when you buy consignment items, antiques, or estate sale things, not only are you getting the item you purchased, but you are also receiving all the energies of the previous owners who have attached their personal energy to that item. There are various methods to clear an item of its old energies. One method is to use white sage to clear it. Use the smoke from the sage stick, and surround the item with the healing properties of the sage. As you are doing this, ask that your new item be cleared of all old energies. Another way to clear something is to sweep your hand across the item as if you are wiping away the old energy with a cloth. Say a prayer requesting that the item be cleared of any old and/or unwanted energy.

Our new apartment was on the second floor, and there was a community pool. The kids loved that part. I could afford only a two-bedroom, so the girls had to share a room. They did not seem to mind, as we had our own little family back together and we were happy.

The denim store that I was working for moved to the mall rather quickly. We all worked very hard to make the store appealing. Our goal was to make sure we gave excellent customer service to each client who visited us, and we did. Unfortunately, the denim store just never seemed to take off, as a big-name chain denim store moved into the mall at the same exact time. They just crushed our business. We closed the store in just four short months. I couldn't believe it. I had come so far, and things were actually looking up. Now what would I do?

I called Naomi. I always called Naomi when I had a problem that I could not solve myself. She always knew how to advise me. She told me not to worry; people who worried, she said, never got anywhere. She taught me that whatever intention you put out to the Universe is what you get back. She explained that God gives you only what you asked for. Well, I did not ask for this. I had negative thoughts racing through my head, like what was I going to do now? She said that I should not worry but should trust in God. I did not listen. I mean, I heard her, but how was this the answer? She told me to have faith. But how do you have faith when your world is crumbling down before you? The Bible says:

Now faith is confidence in what we hope
for and assurance about what we do not see.
—Hebrews 11:1

I would have to find another job making enough money to afford rent, utilities, healthcare, and living expenses for my family. I was thinking, this is seriously not happening to me! I have worked my tail off to get to this point in my life! Then the craziest thing happened. God was really watching over me. Even though I had not learned complete faith in God at this point, He was still helping me. He had faith in me!

The owners of the denim store called me in to their office and told me that I had done a terrific job for them and that they were going to pay me three months' severance pay. My full salary! They suggested that I go into real estate. They gave me a name of a person to call to get started in real estate school. They said that I was an exceptional sales person and that they really felt I would make an excellent real estate agent.

What? This was not what I had been expecting at all. I had thought about real estate once or twice before but just shrugged it off: Me, a Realtor? Well, I thought about what they had said to me, and I made the call. The lady whom they put me in touch with was a successful Realtor. She was a super upbeat person and extremely helpful, plus she had high energy. She told me where to go to school and where to go to work once I received my license. OK, is this not divine intervention at its finest? The Lord definitely had a plan for me. I was to receive three months' severance pay from my job. I was hopeful, as my severance pay would allow me to complete school and sell a piece of real estate within the three-month time frame. My contact said that I had enough time to make a sale if I worked hard. So away I went. The Universe presented me with a new career and I accepted. I was going to be a real estate agent!

Chapter 13

Coincidence or Synchronicity?

As you go through your day, do you ever stop to wonder whether things that happen to you are a coincidence— or is it synchronicity? When you begin to pay attention to these events, you will soon come to realize that nothing happens purely by accident. Everything happens as it's supposed to. I know that when I run into someone I have not seen in a long time, it is always for a reason. They oftentimes say, "I was just thinking of you." Think about it: They often have something to share with you that is important. Maybe a mutual friend is ill and you need to call them, or they tell you about their new accountant and you just happen to be looking for one. Is this a coincidence or a synchronized event orchestrated for your benefit by the universal powers that be?

I am sure you have heard someone say, "I was at the right place at the right time, and I met the perfect mate," or "I connected with the right professional and obtained my goals in business. How lucky I am!" Is it luck? When I chose to pay attention, I realized that the coincidences in my life were not just random events. God actually has a plan for me: my life is synchronized. God will put the right person and the right circumstances in your life. It's up to you to make the choice to act upon the opportunity presented to you. Your choices create the course of your life. You have been given the free will to choose.

In their hearts humans plan their course,
but the Lord establishes their steps.
—Proverbs 16:9

Here is a wonderful story of how the Universe works: A friend of mine phoned me, quite upset. She had arrived at the airport to a several-hour delay. We talked for a bit, and she told me she was going to grab a cup of coffee. In the little coffee shop, impatiently waiting for her flight, she met the man of her dreams. Coincidence? These things usually happen when you least expect them and you need them the most. It's being at the right place at the right time. Some people say, "Timing is everything." I believe this is true. When you are on the right path in life, these synchronicities happen more frequently. The Universe is confirming that you are doing well and telling you to stay on your path.

When you are not on the right road, your life does not fall into place as easily as you might like it to. This is God's way of nudging you to change it up. I have had so many of these encounters, I cannot count them all. When a synchronicity happens, I give thanks. I know that it's the Universe confirming that I am on the right road. This is how it felt when I started in the real estate business. God had put me at the best place for me at that time. Here's more of my story . . .

I learned very quickly that real estate was not a cheap business to get into. There was the tuition due upfront for my schooling, and I needed to purchase the books and the supplies required for the courses. When you are ready to take your test to be licensed, you are required to pay a fee to even take the real estate exams. There were two exams to pass in order to receive my license: the state and the national exams. God provided the money I needed with the severance pay that I received from the denim store. It was enough to cover our living expenses and my school and license fees. So I jumped in feet first.

School was intense. We went every day for about eight weeks. The course taught us all of the ins and outs of the real estate business. The course crammed an enormous amount of real estate law and practice into an accelerated class. The positive in this scenario was that the instructor was wonderful. He was a top-notch teacher. He was an elderly gentleman with striking white hair and a large build. He had been in the real estate industry forever. He knew the business community, and everybody seemed to know him too. I was blessed to have this wise teacher as my instructor. This veteran broker taught us about actual real estate practice, the law, and how it was applied. He shared his own real life experiences in the real estate business with the class. He told us many stories that applied to actual practice. He shared various real estate transactions that happened in his years of practice. His energy was good, he was upbeat, and his message was informative. This made all the difference in the world to me; there was meaning in real estate practice. I would help the people in their purchases and sales of property with integrity and skill. When I read the Preamble to the Realtor Code of Ethics I understood why I wanted to sell real estate.

I want to share with you the beginning of our Preamble:

> Under all is the land. Upon its wise utilization and widely allocated ownership depend the survival and growth of free institutions and of our civilization. REALTORS® should recognize that the interests of the nation and its citizens require the highest and best use of the land and the widest distribution of land ownership. They require the creation of adequate housing, the building of functioning cities, the development of productive industries and farms, and the preservation of a healthful environment.[26]

What an art this real estate business was. I loved it! This was great! I really liked real estate and could hardly wait to take the test and become a Realtor. Again, God put me in the right place at the perfect time.

I remember that it was raining that Saturday morning as I drove to take my test. I was very nervous but confident that I knew the material. There were two parts to the test: Theory and Law and the state and the national real estate exams. You had to pass both tests to receive your license. I knew at this point in the process I had no choice but to pass both tests the first time! I couldn't afford to pay to take the exam again. My funds were getting low, and I only had so much time and money before my severance pay ran out. When you don't have any money to take the test twice, you make sure you pass the first time.

My kids were my biggest cheerleaders. They rooted for me to become a Realtor. Well I did pass the test that day, and with flying colors! All of the studying and hard work had paid off for me. Now I just had to sell something so my kids could have a Christmas. The holidays were quickly approaching.

It was early on a Monday morning when I reported to Prudential Real Estate for my first day of class. The company required all new licensees to go through a six-week training course with Prudential before they would let us out on the streets. We also had to make a sale to graduate the course. I kept thinking to myself, "How was I going to sell a house that quickly?" Naomi always told me to have faith in God. I wondered how this was going to work out for me. Having recently moved to the area, I did not know that many people in Albuquerque. The people that I was meeting were all Realtors, my competitors. I kept thinking how was I going to do this? Whom would I sell homes to? Now as I look back at that time, I know the Lord was with me and my girls. I should have had more faith in him and myself. I was just not there yet.

The six weeks of training seemed to whiz by. We had a small close-knit class. Real estate was not as easy as many people imagine. There was much to learn. Our group was comprised of men and women, young and old. I made life-long friends in our small real estate training class. There are many memories from that time in my life. Many of my class-mates are still practicing today.

The class flew by, and before I knew it our group was wrapping up our six-week training program with Prudential. My real estate sales training was almost complete. The only requirement that I lacked to graduate was a sale. I had to sell a property to graduate from Prudential Real Estate School. I said a prayer and asked for help. I did my best to have faith that things would work out for me. Every day was spent prospecting for clients. Some of my classmates had friends or family members that they were already working with. I was very nervous about finding clients. How was I going to find people who needed to buy or sell real estate? As each day went by, another classmate had a client to work with. I was getting nervous: Would I ever find anyone to buy or sell real estate? I had to remind myself to have faith.

It was a warm, sunny afternoon in late October in New Mexico. Autumn leaves were falling from the trees as I crossed the parking lot from my training office to the main building. Hurrying along, I ran right into a UPS driver. He said hello, and I, newly programmed in the real estate mode, said, "Do you know of anybody who needs to buy or sell real estate?"

He looked at me kind of strangely and said, "Yes, I do." He had been saving for years to buy a house, and he was ready. I was dumbfounded. I gathered my thoughts and started to ask him questions. Was he qualified with a lender? Where did he want to live? He gave me the answers to all of my questions, and we exchanged phone numbers. I could not believe it! I had my first client. His name was Aaron. Now this is divine intervention at its finest. Maybe having faith was working.

The greatest thing about Aaron was that he was a UPS driver. When I began to sell real estate in New Mexico, there was no GPS on your phone or in your car. Aaron wanted to live on the west side of town. I lived on the east side. My travels had not taken me across the river to the west side very often, so this would be a challenge for me. My job was to search for homes in our database that fit my client's criteria. He picked out the homes that he wanted to visit from the listings that I provided. I would set the appointments with the owners. Aaron suggested we meet at a bagel shop early Saturday morning on the west side of town. I agreed.

I was a bit nervous, as this was the first time I had shown homes to a client. Upon arriving to the bagel shop that morning, I could see through the glass that Aaron was already sitting at a table, reviewing the listings that I had given him. My client, the UPS driver, had carefully mapped out the homes we were to visit in geographical order. I was so relieved. I had been sent the perfect client. After a quick cup of coffee, we jumped in my car with our list.

I learned very quickly that this was the way to go—this system worked perfectly! Aaron was the copilot, and I was the pilot; he read me the directions, and I drove. It's funny how God helps you out when you most need it. From that first day forward, this is how I showed homes to buyers. Their job was to read me the directions, and I would drive to the perspective properties. It worked out perfectly. If I made a wrong turn, it didn't look like I did not know my way around. The cool thing was that the client became involved in the whole buying process. My first client was a gift from above. He set the pace for how I showed homes to buyers for the rest of my real estate career.

I found Aaron the perfect home. We wrote an offer, and I negotiated the deal on his behalf. We agreed upon price and terms that worked for all parties involved. It was a learning process for both of us. I coordinated with the lender and the title company and handled all inspections. I arranged for any necessary repairs to the home per the contract and made sure all was relayed between buyer and seller. We closed the deal, and Aaron moved in and enjoyed his first Christmas in his new home. And I learned to have faith in what I could not see. I was able to buy Christmas presents for my girls.

My real estate career thrived. I became Rookie of the Year for the Albuquerque Board of Realtors and became a very successful real estate broker. I opened my own firm in 2003 and was on the right path. If I had not taken that leap of faith and gone into the real estate business, my life and my daughters' lives would have been completely different today. I had faith that God was leading me in the best direction for my life.

There is one important thing I want you to know that will help as you accumulate wealth in your lifetime. I was blessed to learn this important principle early in my real estate career. A very wise soul taught me that if you help your customers and clients unconditionally, you don't need to worry about the profit that you will make from the deal. Do a good job for

them with pure intent, and the money will always come—
and it always has.

Real estate was the vessel God used. He had set this
whole thing up for me. I realized that having faith means
believing in what you cannot see. This was my first step
toward enlightenment. As all of these events were occurring,
and I was learning many valuable lessons. But there was still
some doubt between sales. I would phone my friend Naomi
once a week and ask her, "What do you think? Will I sell
a house soon?" Naomi was a great teacher, with a complete
understanding of how the Universe operated. She would say,
"Of course you will, just draw it in." You may wonder what
she meant by "draw it in." It took me a while to figure it out.
I did, however, learn over time what she meant by it. Naomi
was teaching me that if you want something, you have to
focus on bringing it into your life. You must first learn to
have faith and know that you will receive what you're looking
for when you ask. The key is to be patient and know that you
will receive what you are searching for only when it's time
and not before. You must know how it feels. There has to be
desire in your heart. This is a big lesson for all of us to understand. You can draw something to you, but you must possess
the faith in God and yourself to know that you will receive
it. With the energy of faith comes an abundance of reward.

Learning to have faith has been a difficult lesson, yet the
most rewarding. The cool thing is that when you let go and
just believe, you get what you wish for. Only then do you
realize that the process is perfectly orchestrated by our Creator. When this happens, then you know that God is with

you, for sure! He's driving the bus. It's up to you whether you want to jump on and enjoy the ride with Him.

Some people think this stuff is just mumbo jumbo, but I know from my experiences that it works! The energy exists for our use, and it's free! You make your own life the way you want it to be. You choose to make your own reality with your beliefs. If you believe that God will help you in your life, He will. You simply have to make your request and have faith that all of your dreams and your prayers will be answered, and they will be.

If you choose to pay attention, you will be pleasantly surprised to see all of the synchronicities in your life. And don't forget to give thanks for them when they come!

Chapter 14

The Energy of Affirmations and Visualizations

As I delved into the real estate world, I realized that there were many seminars offered to our industry. There were many motivational speakers to help grow your real estate business. There were financial planners to assist you when you made the big bucks, organizers to assist you, technology gurus to show you the latest and greatest; the list was endless. The first couple of years I saw wonderful motivational speakers like Zig Ziegler, Tony Robins, and Barbara Bush. I wanted to learn the true secrets of success in the sales industry. I was also interested in what message these successful people were conveying. They all spoke about having a positive attitude in your body language and your speech. I started to hear about positive affirmations and visualizations. What were these affirmations they were talking about? And how do you visualize what you want? How do you stay positive and upbeat all the time in this crazy world we live in?

Affirmations

I researched this new sales technique called "affirmations." I studied many books to understand how this magic works. I learned that affirmations are short sentences that you say out loud, telling the Universe what you want. I realized that the words you say and how you say them are of the utmost importance. Louise Hay was one of the first authors that I read regarding this subject. Her books *You Can Heal Your Life* and *Heal Your Body* had a huge impact on me. I realized from her work that I was definitely on the right track. Affirmations could clear old mental thought patterns. I learned that you have to live in the present moment and that each day is a new day to a wise person. We hold the ability to change our thoughts and, as a result, change our lives. She teaches that you can replace your old thought patterns with new affirmations. This is not magic. The spoken word holds energy. This was not a new concept for me—I remembered that Jesus had talked about the power of the spoken word in the Bible.

"But I tell you that everyone will have to give account on the day of judgment for every empty word they have spoken. For by your words you will be acquitted, and by your words you will be condemned."
—Matthew 12:36–37

I began to understand that whatever you put out to the Universe is what you will receive back. It's karma. If you speak positive words, you will receive a positive outcome. This is what the scriptures are trying to teach us. If you speak negatively, the energy of your words will bounce back to you. It is verbal karma. The same goes for your actions or, should I say, your intention. The Universe gives you exactly what you ask for, so be careful what you say to people or about yourself. Remember your words have POWER! They are full of energy. Do not say, "I will never be successful," or you won't be. Self-defeating words are just that.

When I realized the power of the spoken word, I started to say things like, "I sell real estate immediately and constantly, and I accept the abundance," or "Money flows immediately and constantly to me, and I accept the wealth." I began to say positive affirmations in the car on my way to work. I figured out that you must say your affirmations in the present tense and ask for it NOW! Always believe in your heart and soul that you will receive what you are asking for. You must know in your heart and soul that you will receive your request, and you must be able to imagine the feeling you will have once your goal is achieved. This is key. You have to believe it and feel it in order for your request to materialize.

I continued to say my affirmations. The more I said them, the better my business became. I would say my real estate affirmations at least three to five times daily. When I realized this was working, I created affirmations involving my personal life, for example, "My children are happy and successful." Yes, you can say positive affirmations to help others as long as your intentions are pure and good. Your result will be as powerful as your intention is—in other words, how strong the energy of the intention is.

My daughters would tease me about speaking my goals out loud, but I didn't care, because it was working for me and paying our bills. Now don't get me wrong: the Universe brought me only the business; it was up to me to take care of my customers and close the real estate deals myself. I am a professional and do the best job I possibly can for my clients. As my grandmother used to say to me, "Treat others as you would want to be treated." So, I treated every sale like it was my own home purchase or land sale, and I still do. I became so successful in my real estate practice that I opened my own office and hired an assistant to help me.

As my business grew, so did my energy work. The energy work that I have learned over the years has contributed to my success in business and in my personal life. I have learned how to work with the energy that God has given us to use. These things have changed my life so drastically that I felt the need to share my work with you. Let's begin with how to create your own personal affirmations.

There are many wonderful books written about affirmations that you can use and focus upon. I make up my own affirmations. The subject depends on what is going on in my life at the time. I believe that is what you should try to do also.

The rules are simple in creating affirmations. Pretend you are rubbing a magic lamp and that you are asking a genie for a wish. Here are five simple steps to follow:

1. Tell the Universe out loud what you want to receive. (Put the energy out there!) Write down your affirmations so that you can remember them. I write my affirmations on 3" x 5" cards and stick them in my purse or briefcase when traveling. You should say your affirmations first thing in the morning and before you go to sleep. When you read them before you fall asleep, your subconscious seems to absorb the information. Reading them out loud speeds up the energetic process of manifestation.

2. It is important to be specific with your affirmations. Choose your words wisely. Ask for what you want now! Always work in the present tense, as if it's already yours.

3. I make some of my affirmations rhyme. The rhyming fuels the intention with more power. When your affirmations rhyme, you feel the meaning of the words more intensely, and you can also remember the affirmations more easily and light-heartedly. I have fun saying my affirmations when they rhyme. Here are a couple of my favorites:

> *"I am healthy, wealthy and wise;*
> *I have sparkling blue eyes!"*

> *"Everything is going my way:*
> *I have time to play!"*

> *"All my needs are met.*
> *I am thankful for what I get."*

4. Repeat your affirmation out loud at least three times a day, and mean it! Repeat daily until you receive your wish.

5. Always give thanks to our Creator after you say your affirmation. Be grateful!

If you do not receive what you requested, you will receive something better. I have been pleasantly surprised many times when I received the unexpected. Do not say, "When I get it"; say, "Now that I have received it." You have to act as though you have already been granted your wish. Believe! You have to feel it. Imagine the feeling inside when your wish comes true. The actual feeling is what makes the magic work.

You should read your affirmations often, as it will help you to stay focused on your goal. The energy of writing down on paper what you want to achieve gives the intention power. Look at yourself in the mirror as you say your affirmation. When you do this, it tells your subconscious what you desire. Now your subconscious is working on your affirmation without your even realizing it. Affirmations have the power to transform your life. All you have to do is focus on what you want your life to be like. When your mind starts to drift and bad thoughts come into your head, immediately say a positive affirmation like "I am happy, healthy, wealthy, and wise." You have to retrain your mind to think positive thoughts, and the Universe will grant you your wish. Whatever you are thinking about twenty-four hours a day is who you will become and what your circumstances will be. The Universe is granting your wish. Remember, the Universe was created by

God, and He gives you only what you ask for. Here are some affirmations to help get you started. Good Luck!

"My life is filled with joy, love, and happiness, now and forever."

"Healthy business flows to me constantly, and I am grateful."

"Healthy love flows immediately and constantly to me, and I accept the abundance."

"I am healthy, strong, young, joyful, and prosperous, now and always."

"My children are healthy, happy, and prosperous."

"God is supplying all of my needs."

"I fulfill my destiny."

"I have more than enough."

Visualizations

Another technique that I acquired while attending spiritual classes in New Mexico is the power of visualization. You have to be able to see yourself receiving what you want. It's as simple as that. If you can see it and you can feel it, it's yours. This is what athletes do before the Olympics games. They visualize themselves winning. This behavior has been documented numerous times. Visualization works!

The first thing that I attempted to do was visualize a parking spot at the store. I'd visualize a close one, a spot right up front at the grocery store, the mall, or the doctor's. The

Universe was saving this parking spot just for me. The first time I really believed it would be there for me, it was. Then, after that, it was easy. I just knew with unwavering faith that a special spot would always be waiting for me, and it always is.

I have read that some people credit their spirit guides with this assistance. I have always felt that I am tapping into the energy that God created for our use here on earth. We simply have to know how to utilize this precious gift to create what we desire in our life. Now that you know the energy is available to you, working with it should be fun! You have to already know that what you are visualizing will be there for you. Once you have done this a few times, you will be amazed.

As you see the results of your efforts and how easily it works, you can move on to other requests. You may say to yourself, "I need a red sweater," and all of a sudden, someone will give you the perfect red sweater, or you may walk into a store and see the one you had visualized in your mind right in front of you. Now, oftentimes I will say, "Make sure that the sweater I want is on sale!" and I get that too! You have to tell the Universe exactly what you want. You just need to put the intention out there and know that you will receive your request. Be specific with your request. This is very important. You can ask for anything, and the Universe will find a way to make it materialize for you.

Many books have been written about this subject, but the concept is very simple; people make it more difficult than it is. You almost have to be childlike and believe in what you cannot see, and you must have faith. Read what one of my favorite authors, Venice Bloodworth, has to say regarding attracting what you want and the subconscious mind:

> The law of the subconscious mind is suggestion. The subconscious mind does not think reason, balance, judge or reject. It simply accepts all suggestions furnished by the conscious mind; whether they be good or evil, constructive or destructive. Therefore the secret to success is to store your subconscious mind with desire, ambition, courage, determination, enthusiasm and faith in yourself. Add to these indispensable attributes love for your fellow man and faith in the ultimate good of all things.[27]

You can take these practices and apply them to whatever it is that you desire in your life—a new job, a new boyfriend or girlfriend, whatever you wish. Make your wish list. Get out a piece of paper and write down what you want, exactly what you desire. It's best to write it down. When you put some ink to it, that will make your wishes stick.

I have concluded over time that you really need to be specific when you are asking the Universe for something. You have to be careful what you ask for, paying close attention to the spoken or written word. I cannot emphasize this enough. After learning these principles, I was very precise when I asked for something or someone important in my life. Today I am extremely clear in my requests. I choose my words more carefully. When I had asked for things in the past, I'd not paid enough attention to my words. The result that I received was just what I asked for, but it was not what I had intended. You cannot be off the cuff with your request to the Universe; you have to ask for precisely what you want to obtain and achieve. Another lessoned learned.

When I was looking for a relationship, I wrote something like, "Dear God, bring me a wonderful man who is handsome, smart, funny, and religious, and a hard worker like me. Please make sure he loves me for what's on the inside as well as the outside." I was very specific, and this time I received my wish.

Here's an example: If you are looking for a new job, be very clear when requesting a new position. Ask for the location you want to work at, the amount of pay you want to earn, and the hours you would like to work. Be as specific as possible when making your request. You can ask that the boss and other employees be enjoyable to work with. You can add things such as make sure that the employees pull their own weight. See yourself in the new position as successful and making the money you want. Do not underestimate yourself. Remember, the Lord gives you only what is best for you, so if what you are asking for is not in your best interest, you will not receive it.

Visualizations work only with good intentions. You cannot ask the Universe for someone to fail and expect that to happen. This will backfire, and you will fail. Remember that karmic energy is real and that the Universe will respond accordingly. When you do get that new job that you ask for or that fabulous relationship that you have visualized, it's up to you to work at it and keep it.

When you visualize something that you want, like a car, for example, you have to see yourself receiving the car and driving it, and you have to feel what it's like to be behind the wheel. Know what color the car is, what the interior looks like. Do not visualize yourself in the passenger seat, or your friend will get the car! Make sense? The Universe gives you only what you asked for.

Many people have vision boards in their home and/or offices. I learned about vision boards early on. This is how they work: You can use a piece of cardboard, or you can buy a bulletin board if you wish. You place pictures on the board of where you would like to go on vacation, for example, or a picture of your dream home. Maybe you want a new car or want to get married. After selecting your intention, paste the pictures on the board so that you can see them every day. It is a representation of what you would like your future to be. You are putting the intention out to the Universe. You're putting in your request.

For example, if it's money and success you are striving for, then that is what you would place on your vision board. The idea is to look at your board daily. When you are aware of your goals, so is your subconscious. The energy message that you are sending to the Universe from your board is "This is what I want my life to look like." You are drawing in what is important to you in your life. Seeing it every day gets the message into your head; it's subliminal. So now your subconscious understands what you are asking for, and the Universe picks up on that energy, too. That's why when you get into a funk and think only negative thoughts and emotions, your life events go badly. Because of this negative energy, the Universe perceives that that's what you want. The Universe gives you back what you are requesting. So if the energy that you are sending out is negative, that is what you will receive back. It is very important to remember that you get only what you ask for and feel worthy of. It can be a vicious circle if you get into a negative energy rut.

Again, to reiterate, you get what you feel you are worthy of and deserve to have. Emotions play a big role in what you receive. If you feel like you don't deserve something, the Universe will pick up on that energy vibe. When I realized this concept, it totally made sense to me, so I created a vision board for myself. I cut out pictures and wrote words and had fun with the concept. I have a vision board today with my request to the Universe in plain sight. Now I look back and giggle at my actions. Before I realized how the Universe operated, I was completely blind to the idea of visual realization.

Before I understood exactly how the Universe worked, I began collecting colorful, interesting maps. I framed them with rustic wooden frames to hang in my home. I have a map of Baja, California, framed on my wall that I purchased on a trip to Mexico. I picked up another awesome map of Jamaica just because I liked the colors of the map. I went on an unexpected trip to Jamaica. Now I realize that the Universe thought that's where I wanted to go because I had hung it on my wall and looked at it every day for a couple of years.

There is much to be appreciated for the art of Feng Shui, the Chinese art of placement. My advice is to be selective when you decorate your space. Your decorating is sending out the perceived energy to the Universe of what you want. I have a wonderful picture of a couple in Paris on my wall. I would really like to go there with my sweetheart one day soon. I am putting the intention out to the Universe. I cannot wait to see the Eiffel Tower up close!

Chapter 15

The Energy of Meditation

FOR THOSE OF YOU who meditate, kudos to you! The energy that you receive while meditating not only soothes the mind, body, and soul, but it also holds great healing power. Introducing this healthy practice into your daily life will forever change you for the better. Meditation will help you develop an inner relaxation, thus creating a more harmonious, healthy, balanced life for yourself. Breathing properly is essential in meditation; as you begin to concentrate on each breath you take, you feel calmer, more relaxed.

Here is an easy way to get started. Choose a room where you feel comfortable. Sit in a comfortable chair with your feet flat on the floor. You can also sit on the floor with your legs crossed in the meditative position, with your arms resting on your thighs and your index figure and thumb touching (the traditional yogic position). Take in a deep breath, hold it while you count to four, then exhale while you count to four.

You should do this at least eight times. As you begin your meditation, you are bringing yourself into center. Continue this breathing pattern throughout your meditation. Deep breathing calms you down and releases stress. We take this simple act of breathing for granted, but our breath is our very source of life. The Mayo Clinic recommends diaphragmatic breathing to treat emphysema. The calming that is associated with breathing techniques is why breathing exercises are taught in childbirth classes—to calm the mother and child at a stressful time.

Meditation was difficult for me to master, as it was hard for me to clear my mind, let alone sit still for any length of time. Sales people are usually categorized as type A personalities. We type As have a tough time slowing the mind and the body, as we tend to be hyper people. A friend and fellow psychic suggested that I follow along with a guided meditation. This allowed me to relax the conscious mind and let go as I was listening to a soothing voice, instead of having my own mind racing at a million miles per hour. I listen to a chakra healing meditation, as I need to heal myself often with the spiritual work that I do. When you meditate, you are drawing in the energy of the Divine from above. The energy that you draw in will heal your body more effectively. I am always surprised at how much information flows into my mind during my thirty-minute session. When you meditate, you will receive important information. Do not discard the information as irrelevant, as all information acquired during meditation is important or you would not be receiving it. This is how the Universal Energy works.

There are numerous guided meditations available on CDs, as well as many free computer downloads available, to keep you on the right track. This is what has worked for me, and it was the best thing I have ever done for myself. I can actually say I am a calmer, more centered person because of meditation. The amount of information that you gather while in a meditative state is priceless. Meditating enhances your psychic abilities. Meditation is similar to dreaming, and you tend to forget the information quickly, so it is helpful to have a journal handy to jot it down.

If you do not have thirty minutes to meditate in the morning, take an additional fifteen minutes at lunch time. My son-in-law goes out to his car and meditates at his lunch break to clear his mind. He says it rejuvenates him to complete the rest of his day. My husband meditates in the Jacuzzi in the morning because that is what works for him. You need to do what works for you. Begin by meditating for ten minutes a day. I guarantee you that somehow you will find more time to meditate as you begin to reap the benefits of this ancient practice.

The Dalai Lama says:

What do we understand by meditation? From the Buddhist point of view, meditation is a spiritual discipline, one that allows you to have some degree of control over your thoughts and emotions. Why is it that we don't succeed in enjoying the lasting happiness that we are seeking? Buddhism explains that our normal state of mind is such that our thoughts and emotions are wild and unruly, and since we lack the mental discipline needed to tame them, we are powerless to control them. As a result, they control us. And thoughts and emotions, in turn, tend to be controlled by our negative impulses rather than our positive ones. We need to reverse the cycle.[28]

Here is a powerful story about meditation and visualization and how these simple practices have helped change a life. When Rebecca agreed to tell me her story, I was not sure what to expect, as I knew she had had a traumatic event occur in her life that eventually brought her closer to the Lord. Here is her remarkable story.

As a little girl, Rebecca told me she could remember attending church services with her grandmother on Sundays. She explained that she comes from a wonderful family. She has loving parents who were married young and are still together today. Her parents were not the religious type and did not attend church services except on holidays. Her father's mom was a devoted Christian, while her mother's side was of the Jewish faith. When her grandmother's church was sold, she did not attend the new church, and so the visits to church with her grandmother ceased.

When Rebecca was older and attending high school, she joined a youth group and loved it! She said that there was a sense of community and that she felt that she belonged. Rebecca explained to me that she had always wanted to learn more about God but had dark thoughts that often creeped into her head. The negativity seemed to always be with her no matter how happy she was in her life. She was consumed by darkness and experienced terrible nightmares for as long as she could recall. Rebecca had fearful thoughts that entered her head daily, even though on the outside she seemed perfectly happy. And for the most part, she was happy.

While Rebecca was in high school, a horrific tragedy occurred in her life. Her best friend's parents died within a short time of each other, one from cancer and the other one, murdered. As a result, she became angry at God for allowing this to happen. She told me she did not turn to her faith, because she did not have faith at this point in her life. She said she wanted to believe in a Higher Power but was still haunted by her negative thoughts and dreams.

Rebecca moved forward in her life, pushing the negativity down somewhere inside of her. When she was twenty-two and ready to graduate from college as a speech therapist, she had a friend who was also graduating. Her friend and her friend's family were missionaries and were preparing to travel to Ethiopia. The journey would be to an orphanage, where they would teach the children math, reading skills, and about God. Rebecca had a deep desire to go with them. She told me she felt a yearning inside to go and help. Intuitively she felt that she needed this experience in her life. Her parents were not thrilled with the idea of their young daughter traveling to an underdeveloped country for a month or more. She had always worked and saved her own money, and she was of age, so she decided to take the leap and go to Ethiopia. Her friends left on the trip, and Rebecca ended up traveling to the country alone after she attended her sister's wedding, which she didn't want to miss. Her friends would be waiting for her when she arrived.

When she finally reached the orphanage, she realized that this trip was not about her at all; it was all about the kids. She said that although the majority of the children's parents had been stricken with the AIDS virus, they were the happiest children she had ever seen. They had nothing but belief in the Lord and were grateful with all their hearts for their lives. This was not what she had envisioned, but instead she discovered a beautiful culture. The Ethiopian people barely had food, clothing, or shelter, but they were the happiest and the most joyous people she had ever encountered. Rebecca shared with me that many of the children lived at the orphanage but that many did not and would come on their own to worship with Rebecca and her friends.

This experience had such an impact on Rebecca's life that when she started graduate school in the fall, she decided to go to church. She memorized the Lord's Prayer but did not understand the Bible. She said that her nightmares continued with no relief. Although she was attending a Christian church, she told me that she did not feel worthy to be a Christian. There was so much darkness inside of her. She was a prisoner of her own thoughts. She lived in constant fear of everything. She finally told me why: As a young child at the age of four, she had a traumatic experience. The neighbor's son had broken into her family's home in the middle of the night and molested her while her parents and siblings were asleep. Nobody heard the man enter the home or any noise coming from her bedroom.

Rebecca told her parents what had happened to her. They immediately confronted the neighbor family and demanded that the son, who was of age, move out within twenty-four hours or they would alert the authorities. The family did as Rebecca's parents had requested, and no charges were brought. Rebecca explained that her parents had not wanted to put her through any more trauma and that that was why they handled the situation in this manner. She told me that her parents had thought that she was too young at the time to remember and that she had forgotten what had happened to her.

It wasn't until after she had met the man of her dreams that Rebecca decided she needed some help. This wonderful man's family was religious and quite active in the local church. She attended services with his family and requested to be baptized the day before they married, as she felt this would bind their marriage in the eyes of God.

They had been married only two years when she became overweight. The dark thoughts had not left her, and the food comforted her after the bad dreams. She told her husband what had happened to her when she was a little girl, and when he suggested counseling, she agreed to go. They found a counselor and were awaiting her first session when she heard about a meditation class that was being offered. Although she had never meditated before, she signed up to attend, and her husband said he would go with her. The same week that she started counseling, she also began meditation class. She said finding counseling and meditation at the same time was so well orchestrated that she could not believe it. Coincidence?

The counselor turned out to be the perfect person for her. During her first visit, the counselor assured her that she was not damaged in any way and that what she was experiencing was posttraumatic stress disorder, or PTSD. After twenty-four years of suffering, she now realized that she could be helped. She said talking about her traumatic experience changed her life.

She enjoyed the meditation class but had some difficulty focusing, because when she closed her eyes, the negative thoughts seemed to creep into her head. She told me that after a couple of classes, her instructor said, "Oh, and by the way, you can do what's called a hooded-eye during meditation if you have issues closing your eyes completely." She explained that this is often what people with PTSD do in order to be able to meditate. Rebecca just sat in her class dumbfounded, wondering how the teacher had known that this was her issue. Her teacher could have had no idea that Rebecca had this disorder, for Rebecca had only recently found out herself. Wow! Now she could meditate and not close her eyes.

Her counselor called this "eye movement desensitization and reprocessing," or EMDR. This is a fairly new type of psychotherapy. EMDR uses a patient's own rapid rhythmic eye movements, which depress the power of emotionally charged memories of past traumatic events. The teacher went on to say that if you have PTSD, you should never close your eyes completely while meditating.

After much time in counseling, Rebecca was referred to a specialist for her disorder. Rebecca was not happy with this move, as she had become fond of her therapist. Reluctantly, she went to her appointment. The new counselor, a woman, had Rebecca go through a series of visualizations. The counselor asked Rebecca to recall the tragic event and to hold the vision of what had occurred in her bedroom when she was age four. She had difficulty. After the first session, Rebecca did not want to go to her next appointment, but she made it to the office. The counselor asked her again to visualize what had happened to her. Rebecca could see the outline of her attacker standing beside her bed, just as she had hundreds of times throughout her life in her nightmares. She finally gave in and saw him fully, and she began to sob. She let it out; she released it. Finally, she was releasing the hurt and pain that she had held on to for twenty-four years.

As Rebecca continued with her visualizations, she could see a different man holding her. Rebecca told me that she was above her body looking down, and she saw that Jesus was holding her in his arms. This was an out-of-body experience for her. Jesus said to her, "I am here, and I have always been here, Rebecca." God had not turned his back on her as she had thought. She was worthy of the Lord's love. She had turned her back on Him in anger. Rebecca had blamed Him for what had happened to her. After her visualization of Jesus holding her, she felt a sense of calmness inside herself. She had given so much power to this event in her life, and now she had taken her power back. It no longer belonged to the man who had crept into her bedroom that night. The Lord gave it back to Rebecca.

The day I interviewed Rebecca, she told me that she was a completely different person. Her weight had come off, as she works out regularly, and she attends church every Sunday with her husband. And yes, she meditates daily. She told me that she is no longer a victim of what happened to her. This horrific event in her life has shaped who she is, and now she is closer to the Lord than she could ever have imagined. She revealed to me that when a negative thought comes into her head, she sends it out the window. She told me her ears are her windows and she sends the bad thoughts out! She shared that her ultimate goal is to be an example to her family, and her wish is that they find the Lord as she has. Below is the Bible verse that Rebecca uses in her meditations.

May these words of my mouth and this meditation of my heart
be pleasing in your sight,
Lord, my Rock and my Redeemer.
—Psalm 19:14

Chapter 16

The Energy of Love

THERE HAVE BEEN MANY songs written about love. The Beatles tune "All You Need is Love" is one that often comes to mind when I think of how many people are searching for fulfillment. It seems we are all searching for happiness in our materialistic world. If you search long enough, you will realize that love is what you're looking for.

As I am out and about connecting with people, I don't see many smiles on people's faces. Why is this? I feel that many of us are caught up in our fast-paced life and are not noticing that there are people all around us, searching for the same thing we are. Are we all in our own little worlds so much that we are not seeing each other? I often wonder how the joy got lost in some folks. Why don't they smile? I have witnessed people looking down as they text in the supermarket line or crossing off the items on their list. No one looks up and speaks to each other, let alone flashes a smile. What's

the deal? Where's the love? Have we become that discon-
nected? It's sad for me to see.

It's a rarity if you see a smile on someone's face out in
public or hear a kind word uttered to a stranger. I just want to
shake those folks who are in line texting and say, "Wake Up!
Don't you get it? There are people all around you who are
in need of your smile, a kind word, your love energy." Here's
some of Mother Teresa's wisdom regarding love: *"I repeat that
it is not what we do, but how much love we put into doing it."*[29]

Paying someone a compliment can be a very meaningful
act of kindness. Maybe that person in line is having a bad
day and needs a kind word. A compliment from any human
being, stranger or not, is appreciated. A few kind words can
make someone's day a good one! I realize that you are not
going to like everybody in this world and that they may not
be fond of you, either. What I have come to realize is that
when you are happy and know that you are loved, you give
love freely. The nice thing about love is that it's free and it's
contagious. The more love that you give, the more love you
will receive. This is the law of the Universe.

Let no debt remain outstanding, except the continuing debt to love
one another, for whoever loves others has fulfilled the law. The
commandments, "You shall not commit adultery," "You shall not
murder," "You shall not steal," "You shall not covet," and whatever
other command there may be, are summed up in this one com-
mand: "Love your neighbor as yourself." Love does no harm to a
neighbor. Therefore love is the fulfillment of the law.

—Romans 13:8–10

This lesson is simple: if you want love, you must give the energy of love! The Universe knows when you are giving out love vibrations, and it, in turn, rewards you with love energy. God has engineered it that way. Have you ever hear the saying "You only get what you give"? Giving love starts the love energy flowing. Once the giving of love is in motion, the love energy will flow out into the Universe and return back to you tenfold.

Have you ever noticed a couple that's in love, walking along holding hands, and wondered what their secret is? What they have is not a secret. The concept is simple: when you love unconditionally, then you will receive love unconditionally. If you understand this concept, then you are one of the more fortunate souls on this earth. It's the give and the take, the yin and the yang.

I can remember a time when I was searching for the key to happiness. I assumed (as most of us do) that when you have achieved your next material goals in life, then you will be truly happy! It took me much trial and error to realize that the car or the house—the things—were not fulfilling me as a person. Only love, true love, the love energy, fulfills the human soul completely.

My husband and I are in love with each other. So no matter what is happening in our lives, we know that we always have each other at the end of the day. I know that when we are out in public shopping or out to dine, people notice that sparkle in our eyes when we look at each other. What they are picking up on is our love energy for each other. Many times they notice us and comment on how happy we are, as it is evident that we are a happy couple. It is a good feeling to know that you are loved and that you love someone so much that it shows. The love seems to ooze out of us, and we are bright, happy souls.

On the other side of the spectrum, I see many unhappy people who are just going through the motions and seem lost. There are negative folks out there who do not like happy couples. It's the misery-loves-company scenario. What is going on here on our planet? I believe we are so caught up in our worldly life that we have forgotten what the most important thing is—love. We have become such a materialistic society concerned over money, jobs, and basic living issues that our spiritual side has gotten lost. The only way to overcome these stumbling blocks in life is to send out love energy. Love, and the energy that it holds, possesses the ability to bring joy and laughter into anyone's crazy world.

I want to share with you what I have learned thus far in my lifetime about love. The lesson is that the tough days here on this planet are bearable when you have love in your life. You may be in love with your spouse, a child, a parent, or even a pet who keeps the love alive in you. The key is to keep the love alive inside of you, keep the energy flowing, and allow the magic of love to fill you up. My hope is that we all learn to give love and to receive this precious gift that God has given us. The Dali Lama says this about love: "The foundation of all spiritual practice is love. That you practice this well is my only request. Of course, to be able to do so in all situations will take time, but you should not lose courage. If we wish happiness for mankind, love is the only way."[30]

With all the violence and lack of respect for each other occurring daily in our world, to find our way back to loving each other seems nearly impossible. But we have no choice! If we as the human race do not stop the killing and the hatred toward each other, we will be no more. Our world is at a tipping point. We have a chance to Wake Up! The mission is to send out love energy and watch it grow!

Chapter 17

Live Like You Have an Expiration Date

WE LIVE EVERY DAY not knowing what our expiration date is. We probably don't attach enough importance to this fact, but we all have one. I find it quite interesting that people seem to go through life with the mindset that they will live forever in this body. We go about our days doing things and saying things off the cuff. Would you do or say things differently if you knew that it was your last day here on earth?

You might change your attitude or think more carefully when speaking to others if you knew that your number was up. If it were your last days on earth, what would you do? Would it change how you live today? Maybe you would wake up earlier and be a bit more cheerful. You might even stay up later. You would definitely tell your family and friends how much you love them.

I recently saw a movie, *A Beginner's Guide to Endings*, in which three brothers believe that they are all going to die of the same terrible disease. They had taken an experimental drug in their youth, only to discover later that it was lethal. They believe that their expiration day is almost up. They immediately change how they live: They take more chances in all aspects of their lives, both business and personal. They do all the things that they have always wanted to do but never took the time to. They figure out what is most important to them in life.

I know that all of us say that one day we're going to do this or that. Somehow life seems to get in the way of our dreams; somehow that "to do" list just never happens. My feeling is that you have to make it happen. If you have not seen the movie *The Bucket List*, with Morgan Freeman and Jack Nicholson, you should take the time to watch it. If I have not inspired you to write your bucket list today and start living it now, they will!

We all, at times, take our lives for granted, not realizing what a gift it is to be here in the flesh, to be able to experience life as we do. How fortunate we are to have the ability to smell the aroma of fresh bread baking or to feel warm sand between our toes! All of us get caught up in our daily life with work, school, and relationships. We are all focused on our lives and forget to live for today. This could be your last day here on earth, so live every day like it's your last, and keep in mind that we all have an expiration date. I am not suggesting that you dwell on that fact, but at least come to the realization that we are only visiting here.

Last year I attended a friend's funeral. It was a small service with a fiery minister. He preached about remembering what is important in life. He reminded us to always have faith and to love each other while we are here. He spoke of how important it is to be kind to people, to have integrity, and to be honest human beings. He told us that we will all eventually die and that we should try to make a difference in another person's life while we have the opportunity. He reminded us that making a difference in someone else's life is what you will be rewarded for in heaven. He emphasized that it is not important how much money you have when your life comes to an end or how much stuff you have accumulated along the way; it's what you have done to help your fellow man. The lesson here is not to get caught up in all your worldly possessions accumulated while on planet earth.

I want to share the following poem with you. My sister Judy wrote this while she was in the hospital with leukemia. When I read the poem, I am reminded of what is important in life.

JUDY'S SONG

I thank God every day for every day I'm here,
When sickness attacks your life sometimes, it makes it very clear
That every day does matter, and every day is good,
And small things are important, and doing everything you should
To make someone happy; and pray to the Lord above
That your life will get better, and you will do all things with love,
That you will never take for granted the gifts God has given you.
Be grateful for the small things—
wind, sunshine, roses, clouds and skies of blue.
Never forget who made them, and let you enjoy them all.

When you look at life with great faith, at creatures great and small,
Remember where they came from, and how you came to be,
And then you will be humble and thankful just like me.

—Judy Ann Gibson
February 15, 1950–October 15, 2011

The Bible talks about riches and the kingdom of God in the book of Matthew:

Jesus said to [the young man], "If you would be perfect, go, sell what you possess and give to the poor, and you will have treasure in heaven; and come, follow me." . . .

And Jesus said to his disciples, "Truly, I say to you, only with difficulty will a rich person enter the kingdom of heaven. Again I tell you, it is easier for a camel to go through the eye of a needle than for a rich person to enter the kingdom of God."

—Matthew 19:21, 19:23–24

The minister who spoke at my friend's funeral reminded the group that we all have an expiration date and that we could expire tomorrow.

Chapter 18

Rocks and the Energy They Hold

ROCKS HOLD UNIQUE ENERGIES within them. This is why many of us are attracted to rocks. When visiting the gem and mineral shows, I am like a kid in a candy store. I can feel the strong energy of all the different stones as I walk down the aisles. I believe that everyone can feel the energy; it's just how tuned in you choose to be. Exposed to so many gemstones in one place, you may begin to feel a warm, tingly feeling all over your body. You are experiencing their energy. There is an enormous amount of energy held within the stones.

My utmost fascination has always been with the energy of crystals. Their healing energies have been utilized for thousands of years. I am sure the healing energy is what most of us pick up on intuitively. Many cultures have used crystals for healing purposes and for their sacred ceremonies, such as the Tibetan monks, the Druid priests, and Native Americans. Quartz crystals can do so much for you without your even realizing it. The ancient crystals are a silent power source energizing many things on earth without receiving the recognition they deserve.

As we go about our busy lives, we rarely stop to consider how the computer we use every day contains a crystal to make it function. Tiny crystals could hold the key to massive computer memory in the future, as scientists are working on this very thing. The radio you listen to may be powered by a crystal. These ancient rocks have had a huge impact on our modern civilization. The power in quartz crystal is called *silicon dioxide*. Silicon dioxide becomes electric when heat and/or pressure of any kind is applied to it. The crystals release an electrical charge that can be captured and stored. Because the storage is constant and accurate, we as a society have been able to use the crystals in many technologies, such as lasers, optics, ultrasounds, and communications systems. These crystals are a conduit of energy.

Therefore, it is not surprising that crystals can heal your energy field. Quartz crystals are millions of years old and have been used for healing purposes since long before we invented the watch or the liquid crystal display (LCD) television screen. When you hold a crystal in your hand and meditate on a specific intention, the information that you are sending through meditation thought waves can be held within the crystal and the frequency maintained. The crystal will amplify whatever intention you put out to the Universe and transmit that intention. The energy is similar to radio waves. Isn't that a cool thing to know?

All stones have their own unique healing energy. Every precious stone's energy has a unique healing purpose. I have spent years collecting different stones for various healing properties. Stones can assist with your physical and spiritual health, your financial well-being, and your romantic life, and they can even deter negative energies.

I happened to stop by a gem and mineral store one afternoon to gaze at the stones. I walked into the store and began to look in the glass case at the gems. The woman behind the counter looked at me and said very matter-of-factly, "You have many envious people around you, and they are sending you negative energy." I was stunned that she had picked up on this so quickly. She knew quite a bit about energy and had felt this vibe from me while I was in her store. We had never met before, but she said to me in a very matter-of-fact manner, "There are a lot of jealous people around you, and I feel you need protection." People can send negative vibes to you, as I have spoken about in previous chapters. The saleswoman suggested that I carry black obsidian with me in my purse or, better yet, wear one. I decided I would give it a try. I chose an obsidian stone whose energies felt good to me when I held it in my hand. I plopped it in my purse, and away I went.

Knowing the power of the stones, I should not have been surprised that I recognized a change almost immediately. It repelled the negative energy back to the people sending it out. Now I had learned that the stone obsidian is for protection for sensitive people. The stone repels negativity, pain, and any unwelcome feeling from others. At this point I was intrigued, and I started to read about other stones and what their energy could do. I discovered that many stones can help you. Here are some of my favorite stones and the energy that they hold:

Rose quartz, the "stone of love," is the healing stone for your heart. When you wear a heart pendant made from the stone, it will enhance your love vibrations. The Chinese say that if you place a rose quartz under the bed where a woman sleeps, it will keep her man faithful to her. I have not tried this, but I believe it's a great idea to have one in your bedroom. In fact, placing a nice-sized rose quartz in various rooms in a home can fill the entire home with gentle love energy.

The vibrations from rose quartz are a soothing love vibration. The energy of the stone will enhance one's love of self or for a loved one. Wearing rose quartz will generate calming energies when meeting with people. When you have a tough meeting or you encounter someone in the workplace who is difficult to deal with, wearing the stone will work wonders to keep the energy level calm.

Green calcite is a healing stone for the physical body. It is great for emotional balance and to release stress. This gem brings fresh energy to a room.

Sodalite is a deep blue stone that clears the mind and diminishes your fears. Sodalite enhances insight, intuition, observation, and creativity. Since it reduces stress and anxiety, this stone allows you to see your reality from a higher level and better perspective.

Citrine is yellow in color. It awakens the powers of the imagination, activates the thinking process, and enhances mental clarity. Citrine has the ability to get rid of negativity. This stone attracts prosperity and is one of my favorites to wear.

Moldavite derives from a large meteorite that crashed in the Czech Republic millions of years ago. Scientist have varied theories of its origin: Some say it is a fusion of meteoric material and earthly rock. Some suggest that the material is of extraterrestrial origin. There are accounts that the Holy Grail was carved of this green glass stone. The stone assists in spiritual evolution and spiritual protection and is used with other stones to enhance their energy. It is a very powerful rock. When you hold the stone in your hand, it becomes very warm. You can actually feel the energy—be careful, as it can be intense! You have to be careful not to carry this stone with you too often, as the energy may be too strong. Moldavite also holds an affinity to the heart chakra.

Lapis lazuli, deep blue in color, was worn by the pharaohs of ancient Egypt. This beautiful blue gem is oftentimes called the "royal stone." It carries the vibration of the inner queen or king that is in all of us. Powdered lapis was used as eye shadow by Queen Cleopatra. Known as the "stone of self-knowledge and reflection," lapis lazuli enables you to identify your gifts and abilities, activates the third-eye chakra and psychic centers, and enhances your intuition.

Lapis lazuli, Latin for "stone of heaven," is referenced many times in the Old Testament. It is found in Afghanistan and has been exported to the Mediterranean and South Asia since the Neolithic Age. The stone was used in those times for jewelry and for seals.

> *"Afflicted city, lashed by storms and not comforted,*
> *I will rebuild you with stones of turquoise,*
> *your foundations with lapis lazuli.*
> *I will make your battlements of rubies,*
> *your gates of sparkling jewels,*
> *and all your walls of precious stones."*
> —Isaiah 54:11–12

Cleansing your stones is a must. There are several ways to do this. I like to put mine outside in the sunshine. I set them out and leave them all day to soak up the sun's soothing rays. I feel that this not only cleanses them but also reenergizes the rocks. Another method is to soak them in spring water for twenty-four hours. Sea salt is a quicker method if you are using stones for healing. Some people do not like the salt water, as they feel that it interferes with the energy of the crystals. I personally have had no problems soaking them in sea-salt water thus far.

The energy of the stones will heal your chakras. Here for your reference are the stones that I use for healing each energy center in the body:

Root chakra: hematite

Sacral chakra: carnelian

Solar Plexus chakra: citrine

Heart chakra: rose quartz

Throat chakra: sodalite

Third-eye chakra: tiger-eye

Crown chakra: amethyst

I carry several stones with me. I sometimes think that the security at the airport must look twice at all the rocks in my purse when I pass through. But they have never said a word.

The wall was made of jasper, while the city itself was made of pure gold, yet it was as clear as glass. The foundation stones of the wall of the city were decorated with every kind of jewel: the first was jasper, the second sapphire, the third agate, the fourth emerald, the fifth onyx, the sixth carnelian, the seventh chrysolite, the eighth beryl, the ninth topaz, the tenth chrysoprase, the eleventh jacinth, the twelfth amethyst. The twelve gates were twelve pearls, each gate expertly crafted from a single beautiful pearl. And the city street was pure gold, yet it was as transparent as glass.

—Revelation 21:18−21[31]

Chapter 19

Numbers Have Energy

THERE CAME A POINT where I recognized that the same numbers were appearing repeatedly in different aspects of my life, and I began to question why this was happening. My children had been born on the same day but in different months. I found this quite odd. I then realized that my nephew was born on that same day but in a different month and that my grandson was born on the same day as well. Once I began paying attention to numbers, I noticed that the numbers on my license plate added up to this same number, which also shows up in my checking account number, and on it goes. All of this was too coincidental. I had figured out that this number was important in my life, but what did it really mean, if anything?

Then I started to pay closer attention. I started to realize what the Universe was revealing to me: when I am on the right path, the Universe confirms this by showing me my number. This is confirmation that I am doing the right thing or that the purchase I made was a good one. The numbers show me that I am heading down the right road. I began to pay attention to the total dollar amount at the stores where I shopped, and the numbers that came up as my total would tell me whether my purchase was a good one or not. My same lucky numbers would come up every time my purchase was confirmed to be a good one, and the same negative numbers would appear when I knew I should not have been splurging and buying that extra item that I actually did not need. This is interesting stuff if you are willing to pay attention to the numbers and the energy that they hold.

Here's another twist to what I have discovered about "my number": it has carried on to my children and is recognized in their lives too often to be coincidental. My number is also their unique number. Is this hereditary or coincidental? I believe it is total confirmation of a specific pattern to be recognized by our family. The Universe is alerting us and confirming that these are important events in our lives by revealing to us a specific number. My grandson was born on the same day of the month as my daughters were. This same number is my son-in-law's lucky number and has been since before he met my daughter. The road they live on contains this number. My other daughter has a different number, but it is the same number as my husband's and my wedding anniversary and the day that we met, as well as her son's birthday and time of birth. And on it goes . . .

The study of numbers and their mystique dates back to 500 BC. The Greek philosopher Pythagoras, commonly known as the "father of modern mathematics," said that "numbers are the essence of all life." He may be the first person to have realized that numbers are the very foundation of the Universe. The Greeks regarded Pythagoras as an oracle of truth. He saw numbers as a bridge between body and spirit. He realized that numbers have energy; thus, they have meaning contained within them, each digit containing its own unique qualities and potential experiences. After years of research, he confirmed a direct relationship between the numbers in the dates of our births and our living experiences as human beings. He was also able to prove a relationship between numbers and the letters of the alphabet. After years of experiments, "mathematics of the soul" was clearly shown to exist by using a simple formula. The formula is found in books and on YouTube if you would like to check it out.

The bottom line is that numbers have meaning, real life meaning, and if you start to pay attention to them, you will see clearly what your numbers are showing you. For example, my home address before I got married was 225. The 2s signified that I would have two relationships while living at that particular address. The 5, which represents business, meant that I would do a lot of business while in the home. This was the case when I lived at that address. I had two love relationships in that home and conducted quite of a bit of real estate business.

After I got married, my husband and I needed to rent an apartment for a brief time in another state for his work. He had a big job, and we would be there for several months. The address was 205. This meant that there were two of us (a couple) and that we would both be doing business. Coincidence?

I don't think so. The numbers confirmed to me that we had found the best place for us to live at that time in our lives. The Universe was validating that we were on the right path. This is why I have added this chapter on numbers. I wanted you see what the Universe is showing you about your life if you take the time to notice your numbers.

Your Personal Year

I have a dear friend, Arlene, who is intuitive as well. When I visit her, she always asks me, "What year are you in?" I remind her of my birth date, and she does some figuring in her head and says, for example, "Oh, your personal year number this year is 3. You are to learn to be creative." The way she arrives at this number, and the way you can, too, is to add the day on which you were born, to the month of your birth, together with the year of your last birthday. This final number tells you what "year you are in."

Here's an example: Let's say you were born on the 14th day of February, 1971, and your last birthday was in 2015. So you add together the numerals in the day (14), plus numerals in the month (02), plus the numerals in the year of your last birthday (2015), yielding a sum of 15: $(1 + 4) + (0 + 2) + (2 + 0 + 1 + 5) = 5 + 2 + 8 = 15$. Then, to get the "year you are in," you add together the numerals in that sum (15), yielding $1 + 5 = 6$. You are in a year 6. In this case the number 6, which signifies "commitments," is influencing your experiences in life. On your next birthday, in 2016, the number 7 ("materialization") will influence your year, and so on.

Each new birthday brings a new influence into your life. I always say that your birthday rings in your personal New Year! It's a time to celebrate the lessons you have learned over the past year and to set new goals for the New Year. A new birthday is like a fresh start, a new beginning.

Here is a list of influences for the years. There are many variations of the list, but I use this one.

Year 1: *opportunities*

Year 2: *balance*

Year 3: *creativity*

Year 4: *building foundations*

Year 5: *communications*

Year 6: *commitments*

Year 7: *materialization*

Year 8: *karma*

Year 9: *beginnings, endings*

Your Personality Number

You may have heard people talk about your *personality number*. This number will tell you what your personality characteristics are by using the day of your birth. You can find many books that will give you a thorough personality synopsis based on your number. There are numerous sites online you can visit as well. This is fun to figure out. Once you find your number and read your personality characteristics, you will be surprised to find how accurate the numbers are.

To arrive at your personality number, add up the numerals in your day of birth. If your birthday is on the 28th, for example you would add 2 + 8 = 10, then add 1 + 0 = 1; your personality number would then be 28/1. From this number you can find general information about your life—some of your good qualities, patterns that influence your life, as well as information on a spiritual and an emotional level. You can discover the best career choices, and even romance patterns and influences. Numbers have the ability to reveal quite a bit about you. By paying attention to the numbers, you will have a better understanding of the people close to you in your life. The Universe continues presenting us with numbers; it's up to us to acknowledge the numbers and use them to our benefit.

Here is a fun exercise that you can do while driving down the road: As you travel, pay attention to the license plates in front of you and the signs along the way. Notice how often the same number—your number—comes up along your journey. You will be amazed by how often and consistently your number appears. With the energy of the numbers, the Universe is confirming that you are on the right path.

Numbers in the Bible

God used mathematical law to create the Universe. As you take a look at the numbers in the Bible, it may surprise you. You begin to wonder, is numerology biblical? When you take a look at the numbers used in the Bible, you will begin to see a pattern. There seem to be certain numbers that are used repetitively to show the significance of events and places, confirming the power of the energy of numbers.

Here are some interesting examples that I felt important to share with you.

The Number One

One Flesh
"That is why a man leaves his father and mother and is united to his wife, and they become *one* flesh." —Genesis 2:24

"The two will become *one* flesh." —Ephesians 5:31

One God / One Lord
"The LORD our God, the LORD is *one*." —Deuteronomy 6:4

"There is . . . *one* God and Father of all, who is over all and through all and in all." —Ephesians 4:5

"There is but *one* God, the Father . . . and there is but *one* LORD, Jesus Christ." —1 Corinthians 8:6

One God / One Mediator
"For there is *one* God and *one* mediator between God and mankind, the man Christ Jesus, who gave himself as a ransom for all people. —1 Timothy 2:5

One Hope / One Faith / One Baptism
"You were called to *one* hope when you were called; *one* LORD, *one* faith, *one* baptism." —Ephesians 4:4–5

One Man
"From *one* man he made all the nations."—Acts 17:26

"Sin entered the world through *one* man." —Romans 5:12

One Spirit / One Body
"For we were all baptized by *one* Spirit so as to form *one* body ... and we were all given the *one* Spirit to drink."
—1 Corinthians 12:13

"There is *one* body and *one* Spirit." —Ephesians 4:4

The Number Seven / Seventh
Seven Angels
"And I saw the *seven* angels who stand before God."
—Revelation 8:2

Seven Angels / Seven Bowls
"Then one of the four living creatures gave to the *seven* angels *seven* golden bowls filled with the wrath of God."
—Revelation 15:7

Seven Angels / Seven Plagues
"I saw in heaven another great and marvelous sign: *seven* angels with the *seven* last plagues." —Revelation 15:1

"Out of the temple came the *seven* angels with the *seven* plagues." —Revelation 15:6

"No one could enter the temple until the *seven* plagues of the *seven* angels were completed." —Revelation 15:8

Seven Churches / Seven Golden Lampstands / Seven Stars
"'The mystery of the *seven* stars that you saw in my right hand and of the *seven* golden lampstands is this: The *seven* stars are the angels of the *seven* churches, and the *seven* lampstands are the *seven* churches.'" —Revelation 1:20

Seven Days (flood; Festival of Unleavened Bread; Festival of Tabernacles)

"*Seven* days from now I will send rain on the earth. . . . And after the *seven* days the floodwaters came on the earth."
—Genesis 7:4, 7:10

"'For *seven* days eat bread made without yeast, as I commanded you.'" —Exodus 34:18

"'The LORD's Festival of Tabernacles begins and it lasts for *seven* days.'" —Leviticus 23:34

Seven Lamps

"Then make its *seven* lamps and set them up on it so that they light the space in front of it." —Exodus 25:37

Seven Men (Seven Deacons)

"'Brothers and sisters, choose *seven* men from among you who are known to be full of the Spirit and wisdom.'" —Acts 6:3

Seven Priests

"'Have *seven* priests carry trumpets of rams' horns in front of the ark.'" —Joshua 6:4

"'Take up the ark of the covenant of the LORD and have *seven* priests carry trumpets in front of it.'" —Joshua 6:8

Seven Priests / Seven Trumpets

"The *seven* priests carrying the *seven* trumpets . . . went forward." —Joshua 6:8, 6:13

Seven Seals

"Then I saw in the right hand of him who sat on the throne a scroll with writing on both sides and sealed with *seven* seals." —Revelation 5:1

Seven Spirits (sevenfold Spirit)

"'Grace and peace to you from him who is, and who was, and who is to come, and from the *seven* spirits before his throne.'" —Revelation 1:4

Seven Spirits / Seven Horns / Seven Eyes

"The Lamb had *seven* horns and *seven* eyes, which are the *seven* spirits of God sent out into all the earth." —Revelation 5:6

Seven Times (Jericho; cleansing of leper)

"'March around the city *seven* times.'" —Joshua 6:4

"They got up at daybreak and marched around the city *seven* times in the same manner, except that on that day they circled the city *seven* times." —Joshua 6:15

"*Seven* times he shall sprinkle the one to be cleansed of the defiling disease." —Leviticus 14:7

With his finger [the priest shall] sprinkle some of [the oil] before the LORD *seven* times." —Leviticus 14:16

"Go, wash yourself *seven* times in the Jordan, and your flesh will be restored and you will be cleansed." —2 Kings 5:10

Seven Trumpets / Seven Angels

"And I saw the *seven* angels who stand before God, and *seven* trumpets were given to them." —Revelation 8:2

Seven Years / Seven Times Seven Years (Year of Jubilee)

"[David] had reigned . . . *seven* years in Hebron."
—1 Kings 2:11

"'Count off *seven* sabbath years—*seven times seven* years—so that the *seven* sabbath years amount to a period of forty-nine years.'" —Leviticus 25:8

Seventh Day (sabbath; Jericho)

"By the *seventh* day God had finished the work he had been doing; so on the *seventh* day he rested from all his work. Then God blessed the *seventh* day and made it holy." —Genesis 2:2–3

"'The *seventh* day is a sabbath to the LORD your God. . . . For in six days the LORD made the heavens and the earth, the sea, and all that is in them, but he rested on the *seventh* day.'"
—Exodus 20:9, 20:11

"'On the *seventh* day, march around the city *seven* times.'"
—Joshua 6:4

"On the *seventh* day, they got up at daybreak."
—Joshua 6:15

Seventh Month (Year of Jubilee; Festival of Tabernacles)

"'Then have the trumpet sounded everywhere on the tenth day of the *seventh* month.'" —Leviticus 25:9

"Say to the Israelites: 'On the fifteenth day of the *seventh* month the LORD's Festival of Tabernacles begins.'"
—Leviticus 23:34

Seventh Seal
"When he opened the *seventh* seal, there was silence in heaven for about half an hour." —Revelation 8:1

Seventh Year
"'But in the *seventh* year the land is to have a year of sabbath rest.'" —Leviticus 25:4

The Number Twelve

Twelve Apostles
"These are the names of the *twelve* apostles." —Matthew 10:2

Twelve Disciples / The Twelve
"Jesus called his *twelve* disciples to him and gave them authority to drive out impure spirits and to heal every disease and sickness." —Matthew 10:1

"So the *Twelve* gathered all the disciples together." —Acts 6:2

Twelve Hours
"Jesus answered, 'Are there not *twelve* hours of daylight?'" —John 11:9

Twelve Men
"'Choose *twelve* men from among the people, one from each tribe.'" —Joshua 4:2

Twelve Sons
"Jacob had *twelve* sons." —Genesis 35:22

Twelve Stars

"A great sign appeared in heaven: a woman clothed with the sun, with the moon under her feet and a crown of *twelve* stars on her head." —Revelation 12:1

Twelve Stone Pillars / Twelve Tribes

"[Moses] . . . built an altar at the foot of the mountain and set up *twelve* stone pillars representing the *twelve* tribes of Israel." —Exodus 24:4

Twelve Stones

"'Tell them to take up *twelve* stones from the middle of the Jordan.'" —Joshua 4:3

"Joshua set up the *twelve* stones that had been in the middle of the Jordan at the spot where the priests who carried the ark of the covenant had stood." —Joshua 4:9

"Joshua set up at Gilgal the *twelve* stones they had taken out of the Jordan." —Joshua 4:20

"Elijah took *twelve* stones, one for each of the tribes descended from Jacob." —1 Kings 18:31

Twelve Tribes / Twelve Gates / Twelve Messengers / Twelve Emissaries of the Lamb

"[The holy city, Jerusalem,] was surrounded with a wall, great and high. There were *twelve* gates. Assigned to each gate was a messenger, *twelve* in all. And on the gates were inscribed the names of the *twelve* tribes of Israel's sons. . . . On them were inscribed the names of the *twelve* emissaries of the Lamb." —Revelation 21:12, 21:14[32]

The Number Forty

Forty Days

"'For ... one year for each of the *forty* days you explored the land[,] you will suffer for your sins and know what it is like to have me against you.'" —Numbers 14:34

"After his suffering, [Jesus] presented himself to [His chosen apostles] and gave many convincing proofs that he was alive. He appeared to them over a period of *forty* days and spoke about the kingdom of God." —Acts 1:3

Forty Days / Forty Nights

"I will send rain on the earth for *forty* days and *forty* nights, and I will wipe from the face of the earth every living creature I have made.... And rain fell on the earth *forty* days and *forty* nights." —Genesis 7:4

"And [Moses] stayed on the mountain *forty* days and *forty* nights." —Exodus 24:18

"Strengthened by that food, [Elijah] traveled *forty* days and *forty* nights until he reached Horeb, the mountain of God." —1 Kings 19:8

"After fasting *forty* days and *forty* nights, [Jesus] was hungry." —Matthew 4:2

Forty Years (wandering in wilderness; David's and Solomon's reigns; forty-year cycles of Moses's life)

"'Your children will be shepherds here for *forty* years, suffering for your unfaithfulness, until the last of your bodies lies in the wilderness. For *forty* years ... you will suffer for your sins and know what it is like to have me against you.'" —Numbers 14:33–34

"'This agrees with what is written in the book of the prophets: "Did you bring me sacrifices and offerings *forty* years in the wilderness, people of Israel?"'" —Acts 7:42

"[David] had reigned *forty* years over Israel." —1 Kings 2:11

"Solomon reigned in Jerusalem over all Israel *forty* years." —1 Kings 11:42

"'When Moses was *forty* years old, he decided to visit his own people, the Israelites.'" —Acts 7:23

"'After *forty* years had passed, an angel appeared to Moses in the flames of a burning bush in the desert near Mount Sinai.'" —Acts 7:30

"[Moses] led [the Israelites] out of Egypt and performed wonders and signs in Egypt, at the Red Sea and for *forty* years in the wilderness." —Acts 7:36

Chapter 20

The Energy of the Stars, the Planets, and the Moon

God made two great lights—the greater light to govern the day and the lesser light to govern the night. He also made the stars. God set them in the vault of the sky to give light on the earth, to govern the day and the night, and to separate light from darkness.

—Genesis 1:16–18

The Energy of the Stars

To me as a child growing up on a farm, it seemed we were able to see millions of stars clearly. The light pollution of the modern world had not yet reached our country home. My sisters and I would gaze up in the sky and search for the first star to come into view. We would recite the wishing poem as soon as we spotted the first star: "Star light, star bright, first star I see tonight. I wish I may, I wish I might have the wish I wish tonight."

The stars are a welcome reminder of my childhood living in the country. When you are away from the city, there is less light pollution, and you have the opportunity to see millions of stars shining brightly across the sky. There are approximately four hundred billion stars in the galaxy and five hundred billion galaxies in the universe.

The study of astronomy has been around since before biblical times and continues on today. Here is a scripture that I want to share with you mentioning three constellations:

He is the Maker of the Bear and Orion,
the Pleiades and the constellations of the south.
He performs wonders that cannot be fathomed,
miracles that cannot be counted.
—Job 9:9–10

Stars hold cosmic energy. They produce heat, light, ultraviolet rays, x-rays, and other forms of radiation. Some stars hold more energy than others, and they are the ones that shine the most brightly. When you look at a star in the sky, it's as if you are looking back in time. Because the light from a star can take millions of years to reach us here on earth, it's as if you are seeing that star now as it was then.

The star of Bethlehem is probably the most important star mentioned in the Bible:

After Jesus was born in Bethlehem in Judea, during the time of
King Herod, Magi from the east came to Jerusalem and asked,

"Where is the one who has been born king of the Jews? We saw his star when it rose and have come to worship him."

—Matthew 2:1–2

Astronomy, one of the oldest sciences, was studied by Galileo. He was the first to view the heavens through a telescope. Before the telescope, people would observe the motion of objects with the naked eye. Now we have the Hubble Telescope to bring us into full view of the stars, distant galaxies, and nebulae.

The Energy of the Planets

The study of astrology uses the position of the planets and their movements to figure out the effects they have on us here on earth. The position of the planets when you're born is connected to your personality traits. These relationships are mathematically based and include the sun and the moon. This is where your horoscope comes into play. I began reading my horoscope when I was a teenager, although it was not until I was older that I understood how the planets' energies affect our everyday lives. It seems that the placement of the planets when you were born has a great deal to do with your life path. Your life path is already written for you by God; the planets' energies keep you on the right course.

I have been fortunate to meet many intuitive people along my journey. Every one of them has spoken to me about how the planets' energies affect our lives. One planet that we hear about often is Mercury. When the planet Mercury goes retrograde, its energy affects many aspects of our lives.

Mercury goes retrograde three to four times a year. So what happens when Mercury is in retrograde? It is a time to review and revise your life. Mercury rules how we think. During this time you do not want to sign any contracts if you can help it. You should expect delays, so don't travel unless you have to. Your electronics will go on the blink and cause you issues. There are usually phone issues, computer issues—anything to do with communication. And please don't get married during a Mercury retrograde if you can help it: chances are you will be doing it over! We actually become more right-brain oriented at this time. You will notice things during a retrograde that you had overlooked before. You will be forced to reevaluate, reinvent, reform—you have to redo. Communication, especially over the Internet, will be compromised. You will wonder what happened to that email: is it in cyberspace?

Yes, during Mercury retrograde you will have this happen. You can look up the dates of Mercury retrograde for the year and attempt to plan around them or at least be aware of when the phenomenon is occurring. When you start to pay attention to the planets, you will recognize the patterns and may plan your events accordingly. Often you have to stay on schedule and cannot change an important date. If that's the case, it's how the Universe wants it to be.

The Energy of the Moon

The moon has always intrigued me. I feel that the moon's energy is completely underrated. People rarely go outside to sit under the silvery moon like they used to. I feel that television, movies, video games, and the Internet have contributed enormously to keeping us inside at nighttime. You rarely hear people comment on how wonderful the moon looked last night, do you? I believe that we are missing out on the moon's energy. The moon puts out energy just as the sun does. For example, we know that the moon's energy affects the tides. Tides are caused by the gravity force between the earth and the moon. Because of loss of its orbital energy to gravity from the earth, the moon is gradually moving away from earth. Here's a fun fact for you: Did you know that the moon used to be closer to earth? It used to look three times larger than it does now. Can you imagine how huge the moon must have looked to our ancestors?

What I have come to understand is that moon energy has a much stronger effect on us than most of us realize. If you look at most calendars, you will see the symbols for at least four to six of the monthly phases of the moon (waxing crescent, first quarter, half, full, last quarter, and waning crescent). For a more complete picture, refer to almanacs, which show the phases of the moon on each day of the month, along with the times when the moon rises and sets.

Researchers at the Spiritual Science Research Foundation examined the effect of the moon's energy on human behavior. They concluded that the moon has a definite effect on humans.[33] "The frequencies emanating from the Moon affect the frequencies of the . . . mind of human beings. By 'mind' we mean our feelings, emotions and desires."[34] They go on to tell us:

The moon frequencies are slightly more subtle . . . than the subtle-frequencies of our thoughts but are less subtle than the frequencies of the impressions in our mind. The moon frequencies have the capacity to make the thought frequencies from the impressions in our sub-conscious mind to surface to the conscious mind. Once in the conscious mind we become aware of them.[35]

The moon's fullness and position determine its effects on humans. When there is a new moon, it is a good time to set intentions and entertain new ideas. The full moon has a reputation for assisting us to take action. Full moons are also said to have a strong connection to a rise in the incidence of violent crime and sleep difficulties and in the number of childbirths and accidents. Scientists report they have proven that people go a bit nutty when there is a full moon.

The Universe has made me aware of the moon cycles. I have witnessed firsthand how the energy of a full moon can affect people's behavior. The new moon brings a sense of calm, while a full moon's energy seems to stress people out. I believe that just as the sun provides us with vitamin D, the moon gives us its own needed energy. As a rule, we go inside when darkness falls, and we turn on the artificial light. It's unfortunate that we don't spend enough time outside at night to reap the rewards of the energy of our moon. The lesson here is to spend more time outside to soak up some much-needed moon energy.

While we are on the subject of moons, it is important that I mention *blood moons*, which describe the appearance of the moon during a total lunar eclipse. The appearance of a number of blood moons in recent times is an unusual phenomenon. A rare sequence of four blood moon total lunar eclipses, called a *lunar tetrad*, returned recently on the nights of April 14–15, 2014, then October 7–8, 2014, then April 4, 2015, then September 27–28, 2015. These eclipses coincided with two important Jewish holidays, Passover and Sukkot (Feast of Tabernacles). The April 14–15 Passover blood moon and the October 7–8 Sukkot/Feast of Tabernacles blood moon took place on the exact same dates as they had on Passover and Sukkot/Feast of Tabernacles in 70 AD. Those eclipses had occurred when the Roman army destroyed the Second Jewish Temple and the Masada Military Fortress, effectively ending more than 1,000 years of Jewish rule in the Nation of Israel. Could this be a coincidence? I don't think so. The Bible tells us in scripture that God expects us to watch for the signs in the heavens. These eclipses should not be ignored.

My husband and I were camping in early spring, when he happened to wake up around two o'clock in the morning to see a blood moon outside our window. We were a little freaked out because neither of us had seen anything like this before. The moon was full and seemed larger than normal. It was actually red, a dark, scary color red. It was eerie to see the moon blood red, and the energy that night felt strange, to say the least. My husband said that the hair on the back of his neck stood up as he gazed at the red sphere.

"There will be signs in the sun, moon and stars. On the earth, nations will be in anguish and perplexity at the roaring and tossing of the sea. People will faint from terror, apprehensive of what is coming on the world, for the heavenly bodies will be shaken. At that time they will see the Son of Man coming in a cloud with power and great glory. When these things begin to take place, stand up and lift up your heads, because your redemption is drawing near."

—Luke 21:25–28

Two solar eclipses occurred on holidays in 2015, the first on the March Jewish New Year for Kings, and the second on the September Feast of Trumpets. It seems the signs from the heavens have begun. No one but God the Creator of the Universe knows what the future truly holds.

Man has prophesied for centuries about the end of the world as we see it now and the changes that will take place in the future. They call it the "Age of Aquarius," the age of change, of new beginnings. I am not fearful of these times. I believe it is time for us to Wake Up! We as a society have gotten way off track. As more and more people become conscious and aware of what is truly important in life, they will see that change is necessary for our continued existence here on this planet. If nothing changes, then we are headed for destruction. So welcome the new age of consciousness! When everyone gets it, life will be much more pleasant and fulfilling.

The Energy of the Sun

My home state is New Mexico, where the sun shines 360 days a year. I will tell you from experience that having that much sunshine in your life will make your days much happier. Remember, I grew up in the Midwest. I know what dreary days can do to your mindset. Sunshine gives your day a real boost of natural energy flow!

Our sun has brought us warmth and light for 4.5 billion years; the effects of the energy from the sun have been with us for a long time. Think about how nice it is to wake up with the sun shining and the birds singing: you just feel good. The energy is positive and uplifting. When you walk outside and feel the warmth of the sun's rays on your face, it just makes you smile. This may be one of the reasons that many ancient cultures worshiped this almost perfect sphere.

Our ancestors celebrated summer solstice, the longest day of the year. This spiritual time in summer is still celebrated today by many people. I recognize the summer solstice as an honoring of the sun for all the benefits this sphere provides to us. Have you ever thought about how many benefits the sun provides us with every day?

The energy that comes from the sun produces heat and warms our bodies. Our sun's energy has been used for thousands of years to supply heat to humans for our basic needs. Today clean sunlight energy is transformed into many useful forms: thermal, electric, chemical, mechanical, and more. Solar energy becomes the fuel that energizes our plants. This fuel allows humans and animals to live and to grow. In today's society, sunlight is being converted to electricity using photovoltaic (solar) panels. This clean energy source from solar panels, found now on many homes and buildings, is a positive step forward in cleaning up our earth's atmosphere. Solar panels are a cost-effective way to heat and cool your home and help save the environment. The sun's energy is highly organized and is carried by photons. The earth's biosphere absorbs this energy and then releases it back to the Universe. An enormous amount of the energy on our earth comes from our sun, and let's not forget the much-needed vitamin D that our bodies produce when we expose our bare skin to the sun's rays. God really knew what He was doing when He blessed us with this sphere.

We should recognize and give thanks to the sun as our ancestors did. I am grateful for the warmth and free energy that the sun provides. I am also grateful for its good energy effect that brings my energy level higher.

Chapter 21

The Importance of Diet and Exercise to Keep the Energy Flowing

I WANT TO SHARE with you some interesting facts that I have picked up along the way regarding diet and exercise. I am a true believer in having a healthy diet and some sort of daily exercise. To me, diet, exercise, and love are what keep us healthy and happy into old age. Maintaining these lifestyle habits and mindset is not always easy to accomplish. I notice that the majority of people have a difficult time getting in some type of exercise every day, myself included. It is extremely important to keep the energy flowing in your body. It's very easy to get into a rut and not make the effort, but aren't you worth it? I know that when I work out, I always feel better, not just physically but mentally, too. We seem to get sluggish if we don't get up and get moving once the old, dirty energy becomes stagnant in our bodies. This is not just about weight gain; it's about your overall health. I can remember when Oprah and then the First Lady did their big push to get people moving. They were right on! Your heart, your muscles, your bones, and your brain will thank you. We must stay active.

Don't think I haven't played the workout game, because I have. I have been fortunate enough to have had a personal trainer. I have competed at my local gym in "The Challenge" for bodybuilding and came in in second place in my weight class. I was blessed enough to have an awesome trainer pushing me and showing me what exercises were best for me, along with telling me what foods I should eat. This was a life-changing experience for me. After all the competing and the hard work, I realized that it wasn't over—I would have to continue with this workout regimen for the rest of my life if I wanted to stay perfectly fit and healthy. When you exercise often, your energy level remains high. Get up and get moving every day! This keeps the energy flowing in our bodies.

Just like most of you, when I was younger, I didn't have to worry about weight gain, but I bet it sure would have helped my stress level if I had known then what I know now. I could have changed my diet and implemented exercise as a stress-reliever.

I can recall many mornings in my training days waking up before sunrise and going to the gym. I would usually arrive at the gym around six o'clock in the morning and get my thirty minutes of cardio in before I met with my trainer. I am aware that not everyone can afford a personal trainer, although if you can, it's well worth the money. I was so excited to attend my weekly sessions. After my workout, my breakfast consisted of oatmeal with nuts and 2 percent milk, or egg whites with turkey bacon. This all happened before I drove to the office with bottled water in hand. I was obsessed. Unfortunately, I became too skinny and lost my girly shape. I have learned that you can overdo it. Now I realize, "everything in moderation."

For physical training is of some value, but godliness has value for all things, holding promise for both the present life and the life to come.
—1 Timothy 4:8

I feel that this verse is telling us that if you have a healthy body, you will also have a healthy soul.

After going to the gym for years, I started to slack off a little, and I began to eat some of the foods that I knew I should be avoiding. I stopped my intense workout routine. The newness of my workout regimen had eventually worn off, as all things do. Before long I realized that I had gained fifteen POUNDS! What was this? Who was this person in the mirror? My clothes did not fit. I suddenly remembered what my trainer had replied after I'd asked him how long I'd have to do this workout regimen: "For the rest of your life."

So that's the deal. I learned my lesson. You have to do some sort of exercise every single day to keep the chi flowing and the pounds off! Whether it's walking, running, swimming, biking, hiking, or yoga doesn't matter. As long as you exercise your body, you will live a longer, healthier life. I will also add that when you exercise daily and eat properly, you look healthy and vibrant.

I want to mention one other thing that is a must: take a multivitamin daily! Unfortunately, our food supply is lacking in the necessary vitamins and minerals that our bodies require to live healthy, productive lives. The vegetables and fruits that we have today do not possess the amount of nutrients we require as they once did in our parents' day. It takes a certain amount of specific vitamins and minerals to keep our bodies healthy and our energy levels in check. Holistic doctors get my vote when it comes to healing. They use natural remedies to heal our bodies. Find a holistic doctor in your area, and check out their cure rate; I bet you will be astounded.

God blessed us with our bodies to occupy while we are here on earth. He called the body "our temple," as it houses our soul and it should be honored.

Do you not know that your bodies are temples of the Holy Spirit, who is in you, whom you have received from God? You are not your own; you were bought at a price. Therefore honor God with your bodies.
—1 Corinthians 6:19–20

You have a choice to live a healthy, long life or not. It's totally up to you.

When I say you should be eating healthy foods at every meal, I am referring to lots of fruits, vegetables, fish, berries, and nuts. I stopped eating grains because they were making me sick. After some research I have learned that the grains we have available to us today are not the same as those the early settlers ate. They are now full of pesticides and preservatives. The grains are not natural as they once were. As a result I have turned to the Paleolithic, or "paleo," diet.

If you research the Paleolithic era, you will find that humans began transitioning from a hunter-gatherer lifestyle to farming some ten thousand years ago, marking the end of the era. It makes sense to me that because human genes haven't changed that much since humans began transitioning, we are better adapted to the paleo diet. The paleo diet consists mainly of fish, meats and eggs from grass-fed and/or pasture-raised animals, vegetables, fruit, fungi, roots, and nuts. The diet excludes grains, legumes, dairy products, potatoes, refined salt, refined sugar, and processed oils. This diet has worked for many people. *Note*: Check with your doctor before changing your diet.

There is a significant percentage of people in the United States who are obese. This fact is not a secret, and the cause is not a secret. We choose what we put in our mouths. No one really force-feeds us after the age of two or three, right? So you choose to eat healthily or not. It's important that you read the product labels of any packaged foods you purchase at the grocery store. See what's in each product. Does it contain a large amount of sugar, high-fructose corn syrup, preservatives, or artificial colorings or flavorings? Some of the ingredients that you should avoid are fried foods and soda, which have been proven to be two of the worst things that you can put into your body. The grease and the sugar will slowly take you under.

My advice is to cut down on your sugar intake. If soda is your weakness, work on weaning this sugary drink out of your diet. Too much refined sugar can be like a poison to your body. I suggest using raw sugar or coconut sugar, as they are not refined. Many people these days use stevia, which is a plant-derived sweetener and is noncaloric. Drink water during the week, and then have the soda as your reward on the weekend if you must, but "everything in moderation." This is why the French people are not overweight: they eat all those wonderful pastries and rich foods in moderation. That is the key. The Bible talks about how you should not be a glutton. This was God's way of telling us to eat in moderation.

When I was growing up, my mom often made a fabulous dessert for us to enjoy after dinner. Times were different. We lacked the knowledge that this was not good for us. Today we understand that too much dessert makes us weigh too much. My suggestion is to eat that brownie or piece of pie occasionally. The best thing is to have a cheat day. Take one day out of the week and eat whatever you want. Reward yourself! This way you are not depriving yourself of your food favorites. And you have something to look forward to. It's up to us to want to do what is necessary to be healthy and vibrant. I realize that it's easier for some of us to be motivated than for others, but everybody needs to make a conscious decision to eat healthily and exercise.

I love all the calorie-counters that are available to us today. All you need to do is download an app to your phone and count the calories and carbohydrates in a food you're thinking of eating or in the meal you just ate. And how about all the calorie-counter watches that are on the market today? Many people are using this new technology to stay fit and trim.

Now here is an interesting twist on the new workout watches: My husband bought me one for Christmas this past year. I was so excited to wear it. Unfortunately, after a couple of days it stopped working, so we returned it, and I was given a new workout watch. It lasted about two days before its screen, too, went blank. I have to admit to you that I have extremely high energy, and I think I just kept throwing the watch off with my frequency. I have had problems wearing normal watches, because they stop working after I've worn them for a few days. I know this happens to many of you, too; we just have high frequencies.

To sum it up, we are the example for the young people of today. They will produce future generations of healthy, fit adults. I feel we have a duty to pass the knowledge we have acquired on to our children and grandchildren. It would be nice to know that they have learned from our experiences. So the question arises, is all of this hard work worth it? Yes, I feel it is! You feel better mentally, physically, and spiritually. And you will look more vibrant and alive.

A book that I highly recommend that you read changed my life for the better. It's called *Ancient Secret of the Fountain of Youth* by Peter Kelder (I mentioned this book earlier, in chapter 3). This awesome read is about the five once-secret rites practiced by generations of Tibetan monks. Practicing these rites was rumored to be akin to drinking from the fountain of youth. The book explains how the monks' exercises and healthy eating habits have not only extended their lives but also maintained a balanced mental health for them. This is a great source for exercises to get you started on your healthy path. You will learn some yoga moves that will not only benefit your physical health but will also balance your chakras.

Chapter 22

Angels

ALTHOUGH MUCH HAS BEEN written about angels throughout time, we don't seem to acknowledge their presence. They are mentioned nearly three hundred times throughout the Bible. The Archangel Michael and the Angel Raphael are mentioned by name. There are many documented accounts of angels' existence throughout history. Numerous paintings have been created depicting many different angelic beings. I believe that we all have a guardian angel that helps us with our life's challenges. My feeling is that your guardian angel is with you when you are born and is present to assist your soul to heaven when your body dies.

Angels have always been very near and dear to my heart. When I was a little girl, my parents dressed me up like an angel for the Halloween parade in our little town in Ohio. I had large, expansive wings and a sparkling golden halo above my head. (My father could do wonders with coat hangers.) I was the winner of the contest. I can recall thinking how cool it would be to be an angel and fly around assisting people, protecting them, and performing good deeds. Now, I know that's exactly what they do, but I also know that you have to ask for their help, as we have free will. Many people have learned that their guardian angel can prevent a catastrophe by being by their side in a second. My belief is that our guardian angels are here to assist us throughout our lifetime.

For he will command his angels concerning
you to guard you in all your ways.

—Psalm 91:11

I don't recall when I realized that I could ask the angels for their help, but when I did, it seemed that they were always ready to assist me. This may be a new concept for you, so try to be open-minded. When you ask for their assistance with pure intent, they help you every time. It's truly amazing. I have many stories about angels and how I came to believe. Here's a cute one: My husband and I landed in Detroit Metropolitan Airport late one evening. We caught the shuttle to pick up our rental car. As soon as we hopped onto the shuttle with twenty-five other people, the driver told us that our rental company was out of cars and that they were taking us to another rental company. Everyone just looked at each other and sighed. We soon arrived at the building and stepped to the back of the lengthy line. I said to my husband, "It will be OK; we will get a car." I told him, "I asked the angels for help under my breath when we got in line." My

husband has faith, but in times like this he just looks at me—
you know, with that weird look like, Are you kidding me?

After about forty minutes it was our turn. The girl at the
counter was so nice to us; she said, "We are out of vehicles."
Then she looked at us and said, "I have actually found an
SUV for you to drive. The vehicle is at a better rate than you
had originally booked and an upgrade, too." We paid her and
thanked her profusely. As we left the counter, I noticed her
name tag; it read, "Angel." (These things happen to me all the
time. I think the angels mess with me a little just to see if I am
paying attention.)

Here is a true family story: My niece Holly was in a terrible car accident when she was about eighteen years old. It
was a serious accident, and she was airlifted to the hospital in
critical condition. She went through numerous surgeries on
her legs. She said that she was in horrific pain but conscious.
She told me that out of the corner of her eye she kept seeing
someone standing in her hospital room, but that when she
would turn her head to look at who it was, they had gone.
At first she thought it was the medication, but it continued
throughout her long stay and numerous operations in the
hospital. When she mentioned this to her mother, my sister
turned white as a ghost and said, "I have seen the figure, too."
They felt that it had to be an angel watching over her in her
time of need.

Holly told me recently that she had gone to visit her
father-in-law in the hospital, as he was very ill. While she
was sitting with him, he mentioned that he kept seeing this
figure out of the corner of his eye in his room. Holly looked

at and him and explained, "I am sure it is an angel watching over you as they did me when I was very ill." She said that he immediately understood.

You can communicate with angels just as you communicate with God. I feel that the angels are God's helpers. They are ready to assist us when we call on them. You can speak to the angels as you would to a friend. You can ask for their assistance when you need it. Please remember that the request has to be for your highest good as well as for that of anyone else involved. The angels will help with even the smallest things. If you are late for work, ask that the angels get you there on time. I have done this for years, and it always works; I began to realize that they may be able to manipulate time. I request that they watch over my children when I feel that my children need guidance and support. I will call on the angels and ask that they watch over me and my husband in our travels, as they are God's helpers. The key is to just ask. Do not be afraid or think that your request is not important. All requests are heard and answered. Maybe not always in your time frame, but in God's.

Some years back I found myself lost in a large city. I had flown into the airport late at night and alone, and as I drove away from the airport, there were detours on the roads. I thought I knew the way, but I had gotten turned around. I was lost and started to panic; I was afraid. This incident happened in the days before cars were equipped with GPS systems. Finally, out of pure desperation, I said out loud, "Angels, I need your help! Get me out of here, please!"

Within a few seconds I spotted a familiar road and headed in the right direction. I know they guided me there.

Do not forget to show hospitality to strangers, for by so doing some people have shown hospitality to angels without knowing it.
—Hebrews 13:2

Have you ever had someone show up to help you out of a bind, and then they were gone, never to be seen again? This has happened to me a couple times that I am aware of and to others I have spoken to. Angels will take on different forms in order to assist you in life.

When my kids were little, I worked many hours as a single mom. I would pick up the girls from their afterschool program, cook dinner, deal with homework, give baths, and send them off to bed. I was often exhausted at the end of the workday. One evening I was so tired that I fell asleep on the couch after putting the girls to bed. I was not aware that I had forgotten to lock my front door. This was not like me at all. Suddenly I was awakened by a very loud pounding on the front door. Startled by the loud banging, I jumped up and quickly answered it. There was an older lady with piercing blue eyes standing there. I wasn't completely awake, so I am not even sure what she said to me—wrong home, or something to that effect. I do remember, however, that she had the strangest look in her piercing blue eyes, like "lock your door, Girlfriend." It was the most bizarre thing. I locked and bolted the door behind her and wondered who that was. Then I thought, Someone wanted to make sure we were safe and for me to lock the front door. Thinking back, I realized she must have been an angel looking after us, as I never saw this woman again.

Another time, I was leaving work late one cold and snowy evening. As I was pulling out my office parking lot onto the main road, my car got stuck in the snow. My car was halfway in the road and halfway in the parking lot. Now what was I going to do? Suddenly, out of nowhere, a young man appeared. He just showed up. I mean, he came out of nowhere, in the middle of the snowstorm, and pushed my car out of the snowdrift. He was tall and thin, with a short haircut. He wore a black overcoat and leather gloves to match. After he pushed me out, I turned to thank him, but he was already gone just as quickly as he had appeared. Angels are always with you and available to help you when you need them. You just need to make a request and believe. It's important to acknowledge the help they give to you and to always thank them. Gratitude is very important energy, and the angels love gratitude, too.

I am extremely fond of Archangel Michael. He is the warrior angel according to the Bible. I always say I am a warrior because I have hung in there through good times and bad and I still have a good fighting spirit. This is why I can relate to him.

Then war broke out in heaven. Michael and his angels fought against the dragon, and the dragon and his angels fought back. But he was not strong enough, and they lost their place in heaven. The great dragon was hurled down—that ancient

serpent called the devil, or Satan, who leads the whole world
astray. He was hurled to the earth, and his angels with him.
—Revelation 12:7–9

This verse from Revelation clearly demonstrates to the world what a warrior Archangel Michael is. Since I feel most comfortable with Michael, I call on him if I am going to be in a tough situation.

One morning I was driving to work, and I felt like I needed protection from all of the negativity in the world. I called on Archangel Michael and asked him to watch over me. It hadn't been five or ten minutes since I asked out loud for extra protection that I felt my car coming to a screeching halt. The car in front of me had stopped abruptly, and I just did not see the brake lights. My car stopped before I could even put my foot on the pedal. I was rattled, but everything was fine. I thought, "What just happened to me? My prayer was answered, and that quickly?" It startled me. The angels are God's helpers, and they are ready to assist us when we call on them. They saw my near-accident coming and stopped my car for me. When you have things like this occur frequently, you begin to understand that you are not alone. You begin asking for assistance, and you will receive it.

The Angel Gabriel is also mentioned in the scripture as a messenger for God:

The angel said to him, "I am Gabriel. I stand in the presence of God,
and I have been sent to speak to you and to tell you this good news."
—Luke 1:19

Here is another wonderful story confirming the presence of angelic beings: My husband and I live on a lake and were in need of a new boat. As we were driving home from shopping one Saturday afternoon, my husband suggested we stop at the local boat shop to see if they had a vessel that fit our needs. We entered the shop and met a kind and accommodating elderly gentleman named Harry, who owned the shop. We followed him out into his boatyard to view the inventory.

My husband, having spent many years racing jet boats, thought that he and Harry might have crossed paths over the years. As we talked further, Harry said it was possible that they had met since he had been in the marine business for more than fifty years. He proceeded to tell us that he was fortunate to even be alive and speaking with us today. He explained that he had gone through a triple-bypass surgery some years back, which was successful, and he had recovered nicely. Later he found out that his prescribed medication of an aspirin per day along with a blood thinner had been an almost lethal combination for him, but he felt that God must have had more for him to do here on earth. He then asked if we were interested in hearing his story.

Harry proceeded to tell us that he had been eating dinner with his wife at a restaurant one evening when he was struck by an excruciating pain in his head. He told his wife that there was something terribly wrong and that he needed to go to the hospital immediately. She helped him out of the restaurant to the car and rushed him to the emergency room. He said that he was in the back seat of the car in the fetal position because the pain was more than he could bear. He remembers being sedated for testing and eventually waking up in his hospital room.

The doctors explained to him that the aspirin and the blood thinners had caused a weakening of the blood vessels in his brain. Dangerous bleeding in his brain had occurred, which was the cause of his severe pain. The doctors explained that surgery on his brain had been scheduled for the next morning to alleviate the problem. The surgeon who was to perform the brain operation was considered to be the best in his field. He was from Australia on a special exchange program here in the United States. This was quite a rare coincidental occurrence for their small-town hospital.

Harry's wife was exhausted and went home for the night to rest before returning in the morning. As Harry lay there pondering the surgery scheduled in the morning, a male nurse entered his room. The nurse said that he had come to check on Harry and asked if he could sit with Harry awhile. Harry was still in some pain and anxious about the operation, but he accepted. The nurse spoke to Harry about the Lord and asked to pray with him. After their prayer, the nurse explained that the surgeon was one of the best in his field. He said that Harry should not worry or be fearful, as the operation would go well. As Harry drifted off to sleep that night, he felt at peace.

Morning seemed to arrive quickly, and before Harry knew it, he was heading down the hall for brain surgery. He told us that he had not been apprehensive and that he was at peace when his wife kissed him. When the operation was over and Harry was in the recovery room, the famous surgeon from Australia came to let him know that all had gone well. Harry told the surgeon that he had been confident of the surgeon's talents and that the male nurse who had sat with him the night before had assured him of that. The doctor looked at him with a puzzled stare and replied, "We do not have a male nurse on staff at the hospital here, Sir."

Harry had not been sedated the previous evening, and he knew that the man had prayed with him. When he told the doctor that the male nurse had definitely been with him the night before, the doctor just shook his head. After Harry's release from the hospital, he discussed with his wife what had happened to him. They both agreed that the man had to have been an angel sent to assure him that the Lord was with him in his time of need.

> *God sent the angel Gabriel . . . to a virgin pledged to be married to a man named Joseph, a descendant of David. The virgin's name was Mary. The angel went to her and said, "Greetings, you who are highly favored! The Lord is with you."*
>
> —Luke 1:26–28

In Daniel 9:21, Gabriel is described as "the man [Daniel] had seen in the earlier vision" who came to Daniel "in swift flight." It is important to know that the Angel Gabriel interpreted Daniel's visions. One more interesting fact is that Gabriel is the angel who announced the birth of John the Baptist. Gabriel is truly God's messenger. The name "Gabriel" means "God is my strength."

There are many wonderful books in which you can read about angels, but I would just start by recognizing that angels are with us and establishing your own relationship with them. You will be amazed by the assistance they will give to you if you request their help. I feel that the angels are very hard at work on earth right now helping us to establish a higher consciousness. Given how we have gotten so materialistic and full of ego, they are trying even harder to show us that our soul's evolution to a spiritual awareness, rather than material need, is the most important thing to accomplish in this lifetime. My research, along with my intuition, has led me to believe that we are on this planet to evolve our souls. God is not interested in how much money and how many things you have accumulated or how great your physical appearance is. What truly matters is if you have developed the inner you. Have you worked on being kind and forgiving? How many people have you helped along your journey here on earth? I believe that angels are evolved souls and that they are helping us to evolve into better souls ourselves.

Chapter 23

How to Put the Energy to Work for You

LOOKING BACK, I AM grateful for all the lessons that the Lord has shown me. I am looking forward to the many new lessons yet to be learned in this lifetime. I wish I had known these principles a little sooner; however, I have been given the opportunity to teach others about the energy and how to use it for their benefit. My own daughters use these universal lessons as I taught them in their everyday lives. They are aware of the energy, and they pay attention to it. When you know the rules of the game, it is easier to play and be a winner. Knowing and understanding this information affirms any reservations about being on the right path or making the best decisions in your life. I believe that all people are looking for confirmation that they are making the best choices for themselves—validation that they are making the best decisions in their love lives, for their children, and in their careers. The energy flow of the earth gives us the verification that we are looking for, if we choose to pay attention.

Unfortunately, this energy stuff is not something you would normally learn from your parents or in school. That is why I wrote this book. I want to share with you what I have learned so that you may use this information to benefit your life. As people were coming to me for spiritual advice, I realized that I was teaching our Creator's principles to them naturally. It seemed that no matter what the issue they were having in their lives, these principles applied. As each person explained their challenges to me, I realized that they had no idea how the energy works, how God works, or how they could alter challenges in their lives easily. Once I explained to my clients how the Universe operates, they understood. With this knowledge we are able to navigate through life with more confidence.

We were designed to be a spiritual people, a people who recognize the signs that the Universe shows us. God blessed us with intuition so that we know in our soul what is right or wrong. We appear to have lost our spiritual way. We have been concentrating on fulfilling our own needs or whims instead of doing for others. The focus in the world has been on acquiring wealth and material possessions instead of on helping each other. Possibly it has happened over time, or maybe it's always been like this; I am not sure. People are trying to obtain material possessions and community status to make themselves happy. People are looking outside of themselves. They are spending the majority of their time on how they look to others. Who really cares? At the end of your life, when you look back on your journey, how you look or what you have or what other people think of your choices really does not matter at all.

I was guilty of this myself, concerned only with appearances, until I had all the things I wanted and yet I was still not fulfilled. It was a real Wake Up! call to realize that being successful and having lots of money and stuff do not bring true happiness. The ego, it seems, is winning in this world we live in today. We have forgotten the spiritual side of ourselves. How did this happen? Has the media influenced our society that dramatically? Sadly, we have been shown by our television, movies, and print alike that we are supposed to be thin and wealthy and have many worldly possessions and that when we have accomplished all of this, we will be happy. This is not what God intended for His children!

As a society we are not nice to each other. I witness bad behavior everywhere: people just aren't considerate of each other, what with family gossiping about family, friends stabbing each other in the back, and bullying and shootings going on in schools. There is so much negative energy caused by our inflated egos and our craving for material goods.

It is as if our life is a competition. Don't get me wrong: I like to win, too. But know that winning and acquiring stuff make you happy for only a brief period. This feeling is short-lived. There is no substance in money and things. As time passes in your life, you may start to search for something to fill that empty space inside of yourself. What you are searching for is love. Love and light energy are who we really are.

The ego sees love as something that comes from outside itself. It sees the energy of love as something that needs to be conquered or won. The ego views love as a weapon of power used to gain control over others. True love for each other has no expectations. It is given freely and received freely—no expectations, no reward, unselfish love.

One of my favorite scriptures in the Bible is 1 Corinthians 13:4–13. These words were written thousands of years ago and have made a huge impression on many people, including me. I am sure many of you have read this passage from the Bible or heard it spoken at a wedding. If you have not—or even if you have—please take the time now to read it, even if it's once more. This is the real meaning of *Love*:

Love is patient, love is kind. It does not envy, it does not boast, it is not proud. It does not dishonor others, it is not self-seeking, it is not easily angered, it keeps no record of wrongs. Love does not delight in evil but rejoices with the truth. It always protects, always trusts, always hopes, always perseveres.

Love never fails. But where there are prophecies, they will cease; where there are tongues, they will be stilled; where there is knowledge, it will pass away. For we know in part and we prophesy in part, but when completeness comes, what is in part disappears. When I was a child, I talked like a child, I thought like a child, I reasoned like a child. When I became a man, I put the ways of childhood behind me. For now we see only a reflection as in a mirror; then we shall see face to face. Now I know in part; then I shall know fully, even as I am fully known.

And now these three remain: faith, hope and love.
But the greatest of these is love.

—1 Corinthians 13:4–13

We were given guidelines to live by. These guidelines are in the Bible for our reference:

And God spoke all these words:

"I am the Lord your God, who brought you
out of Egypt, out of the land of slavery.

"You shall have no other gods before me.

"You shall not make for yourself an image in the form of any-
thing in heaven above or on the earth beneath or in the waters
below. You shall not bow down to them or worship them;
for I, the Lord your God, am a jealous God, punishing the
children for the sin of the parents to the third and fourth gen-
eration of those who hate me, but showing love to a thousand
generations of those who love me and keep my commandments.

"You shall not misuse the name of the Lord your God, for the Lord
will not hold anyone guiltless who misuses his name.

"Remember the Sabbath day by keeping it holy. Six days you
shall labor and do all your work, but the seventh day is a sabbath
to the Lord your God. On it you shall not do any work, neither
you, nor your son or daughter, nor your male or female servant,
nor your animals, nor any foreigner residing in your towns. For
in six days the Lord made the heavens and the earth, the sea, and

213

all that is in them, but he rested on the seventh day. Therefore the Lord blessed the Sabbath day and made it holy.

"Honor your father and your mother, so that you may live long in the land the Lord your God is giving you.

"You shall not murder.

"You shall not commit adultery.

"You shall not steal.

"You shall not give false testimony against your neighbor.

"You shall not covet your neighbor's house. You shall not covet your neighbor's wife, or his male or female servant, his ox or donkey, or anything that belongs to your neighbor."
—Exodus 20:1–17

God told us in His own words many times in the Bible how He set up the Universal Energy. He said that we should love our neighbors, sending out good positive loving energy, and that the same positive loving energy would return to us tenfold. Simply, we are rewarded for doing what is right in life situations. Being honest and giving, loving others, and feeling grateful to the Creator for your life creates good positive energy flow for you.

"'Do not seek revenge or bear a grudge against anyone among your people, but love your neighbor as yourself. I am the Lord.'"
—Leviticus 19:18

It's surprising to me that as long as these universal laws have been in place, they are not recognized and used by all of us. I acknowledge that there is both light and dark in our world; however, I believe that there is an enlightening happening right now! This enlightenment is within people. They are learning there is more to this journey than just the material, superficial world that we are living in today. There are more and more people searching and evolving into spiritual beings.

Numerous biblical movies have been made in the past few years, a development that is nice to see. The old stories that I was taught in Sunday school are being told again. These Bible stories address lessons that God wants us to learn. Today's society continues to repeat the same mistakes that people made in biblical times. I perceive that most people are just going through the motions as if they were zombies or something. Wake Up! Realize what is important in life: your family, your friends, and the people that you encounter every day. This is the secret to true happiness—caring about your fellow man, giving to each other, helping one another, and, most importantly, loving each other.

These words of wisdom from the Dalai Lama sum it up:

> We are all on this planet together. We are all brothers and sisters with the same physical and mental faculties, the same problems, and the same needs. We must all contribute to the fulfillment of the human potential and the improvement of the quality of life as much as we are able. Mankind is crying out for help. Ours is a desperate time. Those

who have something to offer should come forward. Now is the time.[36]

My goal is to raise the vibration on our planet so that we may all live in peace and harmony and learn to work collectively. I believe that we are holding back the Universe as materialism keeps us in this density. *Let's raise the vibration on this planet with our good energy!*

I am excited that I am here on earth to see a change in our consciousness, a shift in the energy. My wish is that I will make a difference in people's lives with my teachings. I am excited to contribute to this spiritual revolution. We are here on earth to learn lessons. I believe that the most important lessons for us to achieve are simple: be grateful you are here, be kind to each other, help one another, love each other, and use the energy for good, as it was intended.

May the Lord Bless you and Keep you.

Notes

All scripture quotations, unless otherwise indicated, are taken from the *Holy Bible, New International Version*®, *NIV*®. Copyright ©1973, 1978, 1984, 2011 by Biblica, Inc.™ Used by permission of Zondervan. All rights reserved worldwide. www.zondervan.com. The "NIV" and "New International Version" are trademarks registered in the United States Patent and Trademark Office by Biblica, Inc.™.

Chapter 2

1. Edgar Cayce, *Auras: An Essay on the Meaning of Colors* (Virginia Beach: A.R.E. Press, 1945), 5. Edgar Cayce Readings © 1971, 1993–2007 by the Edgar Cayce Foundation.

Used by Permission. All Rights Reserved.

2. Ibid.

3. Ibid., 6.

4. Ibid., 15.

Chapter 3

5. Rev. Rosalyn L. Bruyere, *Wheels of Light: Chakras, Auras, and the Healing Energy of the Body* (New York: Fireside, 1994), 18. Copyright © 1989, 1991, 1994, All Rights Reserved.

Healing Light Center Church, accessed October 4, 2016, http://www.rosalynlbruyere.org/.

6. Rhonda Harris-Choudhry, psychic metaphysician, henna artist, and teacher.

Chapter 4
7. Ann Linda Baldwin, Mind-Body-Science, accessed September 28, 2016, http://mind-body-science.com/.

8. Ibid.

9. Ibid.

10. Mitchell L. Gaynor, *The Healing Power of Sound: Recovery from Life-Threatening Illness Using Sound, Voice, and Music* (Boston: Shambhala Publications, 2002), 27.

11. Elivia Melodey, "Spiritual Healing Angels: Vibrational Sound Healing," Hearts with Soul: Gathering of Angels, accessed September 6, 2016, http://www.heartswithsoul.com/elivia_sound.htm.

12. Cayce, *Auras*, 15.

13. Ibid., 20.

Chapter 5
14. Siusaidh McDonald, "The Story of Thieves Oil.....," phpBB: YoungLivingForum.com, Mar. 6, 2009 3:23 p.m., http://younglivingforum.com/viewtopic.php?t=925.

15. Dr. Mark Evans, "The Cancer-Killing Properties of Frankincense in Ovarian Cancer," podcast audio, accessed October 4, 2016, http://soundcloud.com/university-of-leicester/mark-evans; "Christmas Gift Brings Treatment Hope for Cancer Patients," University of Leicester, accessed September 27, 2016, http://www2.le.ac.uk/news/blog/2013/december/christmas-gift-brings-treatment-hope-for-cancer-patients.

16. Mahmoud Suhail, quoted in Jeremy Howell, "Frankincense: Could It Be a Cure for Cancer?," BBC News, last updated 10:59 GMT, February 9, 2010, http://news.bbc.co.uk/2/hi/middle_east/8505251.stm.

17. Steven D. Ehrlich, "Lavender," University of Maryland Medical Center, version info last reviewed January 2, 2015, http://umm.edu/health/medical/altmed/herb/lavender.

18. Valerie Ann Worwood, *The Complete Book of Essential Oils and Aromatherapy* (San Rafael, CA: New World Library, 1991), 2.

Chapter 6

19. "Dietary Reference Intakes for Water, Potassium, Sodium, Chloride, and Sulfate: Panel on Dietary Reference Intakes for Electrolytes and Water," Institute of Medicine of the National Academies (Washington, DC: National Academies Press), accessed September 18, 2016, https://www.nap.edu/read/10925/chapter/4; National Academies of Sciences, Engineering, and Medicine, accessed October 3, 2016, http://nationalacademies.org/.

20. Masaru Emoto, Masaru Emoto's Hado World, accessed September 28, 2016, http://hado.com/ihm/.

21. Ibid.

Chapter 7

22. The Dalai Lama: His Essential Wisdom, ed. Carol Kelly-Gangi (New York: Fall River Press, 2007), 16.

23. Rob Stein, "Prayer's Power to Heal Strangers Is Examined," Washington Post, July 15, 2005, http://www.washingtonpost.com/wp-dyn/content/article/2005/07/14/AR2005071401695.html.

Chapter 9

24. Eldon Taylor, Choices and Illusions: How Did I Get Where I Am, and How Do I Get Where I Want to Be? (Carlsbad, CA: Hay House, 2007), 74.

Chapter 10

25. Dalai Lama, ed. Kelly-Gangi, 46.

Chapter 13

26. "The Preamble to the Code of Ethics," National Association of Realtors®, accessed September 14, 2016, http://www.realtor.org/sites/default/files/policies/2007/code-of-ethics-preamble-2007-11-27.pdf.

Chapter 14

27. Venice J. Bloodworth, Key to Yourself (Memphis: DeVorss Company, 1952), 60.

Chapter 15

28. Dalai Lama, ed. Kelly-Gangi, 56.

Chapter 16

29. Mother Teresa, *Love: The Words and Inspirations of Mother Teresa* (Boulder, CO: Blue Mountain Arts, 2007), 69 (from address delivered in Rome, May 1982). The writings of Mother Teresa of Calcutta © by the Mother Teresa Center, exclusive licensee throughout the world of the Missionaries of Charity for the works of Mother Teresa. Used with permission. Accessed September 28, 2016, www.motherteresa.org.

30. *Dalai Lama*, ed. Kelly-Gangi, 24.

Chapter 18

31. *The Voice Bible*, copyright © 2012 Thomas Nelson, Inc. *The Voice*™ translation © 2012 Ecclesia Bible Society. All rights reserved.

Chapter 19

32. Ibid.

Chapter 20

33. "Effect of the Moon on Man: A Spiritual Perspective," section 1, Spiritual Science Research Foundation, accessed September 9, 2016, http://www.spiritualresearchfoundation.org/spiritual-problems/effects-of-nature-and-environment/new-full-moon-effects/. Copyright © Spiritual Science Research Foundation Inc. (SSRF). Courtesy of SSRF.

34. Ibid., section 2.

35. Ibid.

Chapter 23

36. *Dalai Lama*, ed. Kelly-Gangi, 67.

Bibliography

Baldwin, Ann Linda. Mind-Body-Science. Accessed September 28, 2016. http://mind-body -science.com/.

Bloodworth, Venice J. *Key to Yourself*. Memphis: DeVorss Company, 1952.

Bruyere, Rev. Rosalyn L. *Wheels of Light: Chakras, Auras, and the Healing Energy of the Body*.

New York: Fireside, 1994. Copyright © 1989, 1991, 1994. All Rights Reserved.

Burton, Sarah. "Study Explores Effects of Harp Music on ICU Patients." University of Arizona Medical Center. July 30, 2012. https://uanews.arizona.edu/story/ study-explores-effects-of-harp-music-on-icu-patients.

Cayce, Edgar. *Auras: An Essay on the Meaning of Colors*. Virginia Beach: A.R.E. Press, 1945. Edgar Cayce Readings © 1971, 1993–2007 by the Edgar Cayce Foundation.Used by Permission. All Rights Reserved.

Chiasson, Ann Marie, Ann Linda Baldwin, Carrol McLaughlin, Paula Cook, and Gulshan Sethi.

"The Effect of Live Spontaneous Harp Music on Patients in the Intensive Care Unit."

Evidence-Based Complementary and Alternative Medicine 2013, art. ID 428731. Nov. 12, 2013. https://www.hindawi.com/journals/ ecam/2013/428731/.

"Christmas Gift Brings Treatment Hope for Cancer Patients." University of Leicester Press Office. December 20, 2013.

http://www2.le.ac.uk/news/blog/2013/december /
christmas-gift-brings-treatment-hope-for-cancer-patients.

Dalai Lama, *Dalai Lama: His Essential Wisdom*. Edited by Carol
Kelly-Gangi. New York: Fall River Press, 2007.

"Effect of the Moon on Man: A Spiritual Perspective."
Spiritual Science Research Foundation Inc. Accessed
September 20, 2016. Copyright © Spiritual Science
Research Foundation Inc. All Rights Reserved. http://
www.spiritualresearchfoundation.org/spiritual-problems/
effects-of-nature-and-environment/new-full-moon-effects/.

Ehrlich, Steven D. "Lavender." University of Maryland Medical
Center. Version info last reviewed January 2, 2015. http://
umm.edu/health/medical/altmed/herb/lavender.

Emoto, Masaru. Masaru Emoto's Hado World. Accessed
September 28, 2016. http://hado.com/ihm/.

Evans, Mark. "The Cancer-Killing Properties of Frankincense in
Ovarian Cancer." Podcast audio. Accessed October 4, 2016.
http://soundcloud.com/university-of-leicester/mark-evans.

Gaynor, Mitchell L. *The Healing Power of Sound: Recovery from Life-
Threatening Illness Using Sound, Voice, and Music*. Boston:
Shambhala Publications, 2002.

———. Quoted in "Tibetan Bowls Enhance and Complement
Your Yoga Practice." Diáne Mandle. Sound Energy
Healing. Accessed September 16, 2016. http://www.
soundenergyhealing.com/pages/articles_usingSound.html.

Harp Therapy Int'l. Accessed September 20, 2016. http://www.
harptherapyinternational.com/.

Hay, Louise. *Heal Your Body*. Carlsbad, CA: Hay House Inc., 1988.

———. *You Can Heal Your Life*. Carlsbad, CA: Hay House Inc., 1999.

Higley, Connie and Alan Higley. *Quick Reference Guide for Using
Essential Oils*. Spanish Fork, UT: Abundant Health, 2013.

Holy Bible, New International Version®: Holy Bible, New International Version®, NIV®.

Copyright ©1973, 1978, 1984, 2011. By Biblica, Inc.™ Used by permission of Zondervan. All rights reserved worldwide. www. zondervan.com. The "NIV" and "New International Version" are trademarks registered in the United States Patent and Trademark Office by Biblica, Inc.™.

Kelder, Peter. *Ancient Secret of the Fountain of Youth.* New York: Doubleday Dell   Publishing Group, 1998. Copyright © 1985, 1989, 1998 by Harbor Press.

McDonald, Siusaidh. "The Story of Thieves Oil....." phpBB: YoungLivingForum.com. Mar. 6, 2009 3:23 p.m. http:// younglivingforum.com/viewtopic.php?t=925.

Melodey, Elivia. "Spiritual Healing Angels: Vibrational Sound Healing." Hearts with Soul: Gathering of Angels. Accessed September 6, 2016. http://www.heartswithsoul.com/elivia_sound.htm.

Mercier, Patricia. *The Chakra Bible: The Definitive Guide to Working with Chakras.* New York: Sterling, 2007.

Mother Teresa. *Love: The Words and Inspiration of Mother Teresa.* Boulder, CO: Blue Mountain Arts, 2007.

Mother Teresa Center. The writings of Mother Teresa of Calcutta © by the Mother Teresa Center, exclusive licensee throughout the world of Missionaries of Charity for the works of Mother Teresa. Accessed September 28, 2016. www.motherteresa.org.

Phillips, David A. *The Complete Book of Numerology.* Carlsbad, CA: Hay House, 1992.

"Preamble." Code of Ethics. National Association of Realtors®. Accessed September 14, 2016. http://www.realtor. org/sites/default/files/policies/2007/code-of-ethics-preamble-2007-11-27.pdf.

Simmons, Robert, and Naisha Ahsian. Contributor Hazel Raven. *The Book of Stones: Who They Are and What They Teach*. East Montpelier, VT: Heaven and Earth Publishing, 1998.

Stein, Rob. "Prayer's Power to Heal Strangers Is Examined." *Washington Post*. July 15, 2005. http://www.washingtonpost. com/wp-dyn/content/article/2005/07/14/AR2005071401695. html.

Suhail, Mahmoud. Quoted in Jeremy Howell. "Frankincense: Could It Be a Cure for Cancer?" BBC News. Last updated 10:59 GMT, February 9, 2010. http://news.bbc.co.uk/2/hi/middle_ east/8505251.stm.

Taylor, Eldon. *Choices and Illusions: How Did I Get Where I Am, and How Do I Get Where I Want to Be?* Carlsbad, CA: Hay House, 2007.

Institute of Medicine of the National Academies. "Dietary Reference Intakes for Water,   Potassium, Sodium, Chloride, and Sulfate: Panel on Dietary Reference Intakes for Electrolytes and Water." Washington, DC: National Academies Press. Accessed September 18, 2016. https://www.nap.edu/read/10925/ chapter/4.

Virtue, Doreen. *Chakra Clearing: Awakening Your Spiritual Power to Know and Heal*. Carlsbad, CA: Hay House, 1994–2004.

The Voice Bible. Copyright © 2012 Thomas Nelson, Inc. The Voice™ translation © 2012. Ecclesia Bible Society. All rights reserved.

Worwood, Valerie Ann. *The Complete Book of Essential Oils and Aromatherapy*. San Rafael, CA: New World Library, 1991.

About the Author

Nancy continues her energy work as an author, a spiritual life coach, and a motivational speaker. Her faith in the Lord and her intuitive abilities have enhanced over the years, giving her the necessary skills to assist many people on their spiritual paths. Her belief in the Lord is what ignites her light to do this work.

As Nancy continues on her spiritual path, she maintains her real estate broker license. She has enjoyed a successful career as the owner of her own real estate firm in New Mexico. Her expertise in business has allowed her to assist numerous homeowners and investors successfully for twenty years.

Nancy has also enjoyed an extensive corporate career as a sales coordinator with one of the Big Three automakers in Detroit. Her sales, management, and marketing skills have grown with each step of her business. Her success has blessed her with the real life experience, knowledge, and common sense that is required to help others through life's challenges.

Utilizing both her intuitive and her acquired spiritual education, she has been able to create the life she wants for herself. Now she teaches others how to create what they want in their lives. Her spiritual schooling encompasses numerous energy and spiritual-education classes and workshops over the years. Her teachers in Michigan and New Mexico have proved invaluable to her current energy work. Her path has developed through religious study and the acquisition of information about various cultures and their religious practices. She is a Christian and a member of the Baptist Church.

Nancy has been fortunate to acquire hands-on energy-healing skills from an Aztec healer from Mexico, and she has helped many balance their energy fields. She has received guidance from religious and spiritual teachers along the way, resulting in the development of her skills as an intuitive, a tarot card reader, and a life coach. She utilizes these tools to guide her clients to joyful and successful lives.

As a mom and a grandmother, she enjoys sharing her life experiences in her writings, her private readings, and her talks. She loves numerology and pays attention to the numbers while traveling with her husband, an electrical contractor. They have wonderful children and three grandchildren who light up their lives. To find out more about Nancy's work and to see her latest energy tips, visit her website at www.theenergyprophet.com. For more spiritual insight, you can view Nancy Yearout on YouTube. She writes a fun and informative blog on www.nancyyearout.com.